W9-AXD-116

MARTIN LUTHER KING, JR.

The Dream of Peaceful Revolution

The History of the Civil Rights Movement

ELLA BAKER: A Leader Behind the Scenes

STOKELY CARMICHAEL: The Story of Black Power

FANNIE LOU HAMER: From Sharecropping to Politics

JESSE JACKSON: Still Fighting for the Dream

MARTIN LUTHER KING, JR.: The Dream of Peaceful Revolution

MALCOLM X: Another Side of the Movement

THURGOOD MARSHALL: The Fight for Equal Justice

ROSA PARKS: The Movement Organizes

A. PHILIP RANDOLPH: Integration in the Workplace

MARTIN LUTHER KING, JR.

The Dream of Peaceful Revolution

by **Della Rowland**

With an Introduction by

ANDREW YOUNG

Silver Burdett Press

To the memory and legacy of Martin Luther King, Jr.,
and to the famous and nameless ones
who fight for freedom everywhere.
And to Tony Fradkin—for another kind of freedom.

The author is grateful to Della Cohen, Mark Davies, Richard Gallin, and Aldon Morris for their support and editorial guidance; and to Clark Johnson, Jr., Ora Lee Ogburn, and Michael D. Woodward for loving guidance years ago.

Series Consultant: Aldon Morris

Cover and Text Design: Design Five, New York
Maps: General Cartography, Inc.
Series Editorial Supervisor: Richard G. Gallin
Series Supervision of Art and Design: Leslie Bauman
Series Editing: Agincourt Press
Concept Editor: Della Rowland

Consultants: Dr. Elysa Robinson, COMPACT Coordinator, Detroit Public Schools, Detroit, Michigan; Catherine J. Lenix-Hooker, Deputy Chief, Schomburg Center for Research in Black Culture, New York Public Library, New York City.

Published by Silver Burdett Press, Inc., a division of Simon & Schuster, Inc. Prentice Hall Building, Englewood Cliffs, NJ 07632.

Permissions and photo credits appear on page 138.

Library of Congress Cataloging-in-Publication Data

Rowland, Della.
Martin Luther King., Jr. : the dream of peaceful revolution / by Della Rowland, with an introduction by Andrew Young.
p. cm.—(The History of the civil rights movement)
Includes bibliographical references and index.
Summary: A biography of the Nobel Peace Prize winner who showed us that a struggle can be waged without violence.
1. King, Martin Luther, Jr., 1929–1968—Juvenile literature. 2. Afro-Americans—Biography—Juvenile literature. 3. Civil rights workers—United States—Biography—Juvenile literature. 4. Baptists—United States—Clergy—Biography—Juvenile literature. 5. Afro-Americans—Civil rights—Juvenile literature. 6. Civil rights movements—United States—History—20th century—Juvenile literature. [1. King, Martin Luther, Jr., 1929–1968. 2. Civil rights workers. 3. Afro-Americans—Biography.] I. Title. II. Series.
E185.97.K5R63 1990
323′.092—dc20
[B]
[92] 90-31798
ISBN 0-382-09924-9 (lib. bdg.) CIP
ISBN 0-382-24062-6 (pbk.) AC

CONTENTS

INTRODUCTION

By Andrew Young

Some thirty years ago, a peaceful revolution took place in the United States, as African Americans sought equal rights. That revolution, which occurred between 1954 and 1968, is called the civil rights movement. Actually, African Americans have been struggling for their civil rights for as long as they have been in this country. Before the Civil War, brave abolitionists were calling out for an end to the injustice and cruelty of slavery. Even after the Civil War freed slaves, African Americans were still forced to fight other forms of racism and discrimination—segregation and prejudice. This movement still continues today as people of color battle racial hatred and economic exploitation all over the world.

The books in this series tell the stories of the lives of Ella Baker, Stokely Carmichael, Fannie Lou Hamer, Jesse Jackson, Malcolm X, Thurgood Marshall, Rosa Parks, A. Philip Randolph, and Martin Luther King, Jr.—just a few of the thousands of brave people who worked in the civil rights movement. Learning about these heroes is an important lesson in American history. They risked their homes and their jobs—and some gave their lives—to secure rights and freedoms that we now enjoy and often take for granted.

Most of us know the name of Dr. Martin Luther King, Jr., the nonviolent leader of the movement. But others who were just as important may not be as familiar. Rosa Parks insisted on her right to a seat on a public bus. Her action started a bus boycott that changed a segregation law and sparked a movement.

Ella Baker was instrumental in founding two major civil rights organizations, the Southern Christian Leadership Conference (SCLC) and the Student Nonviolent Coordinating Committee (SNCC). One of the chairpersons of SNCC, Stokely Carmichael, is perhaps best known for making the slogan "Black Power" famous. Malcolm X, the strong voice from the urban north, rose from a prison inmate to a powerful black Muslim leader.

Not many people know that the main organizer of the 1963 March on Washington was A. Philip Randolph. Younger leaders called Randolph the "father of the movement." Fannie Lou Hamer, a poor sharecropper from Mississippi, was such a powerful speaker for voters rights that President Lyndon Johnson blocked out television coverage of the 1964 Democratic National Convention to keep her off the air. Thurgood Marshall was the first African American to be made a Supreme Court justice.

Many who demanded equality paid for their actions. They were fired from their jobs, thrown out of their homes, beaten, and even killed. But they marched, went to jail, and put their lives on the line over and over again for the right to equal justice. These rights include something as simple as being able to sit and eat at a lunch counter. They include political rights such as the right to vote. They also include the equal rights to education and job opportunities that lead to economic betterment.

We are now approaching a level of democracy that allows all citizens of the United States to participate in the American dream. Jesse Jackson, for example, has pursued the dream of the highest office in this land, the president of the United States. Jackson's running for president was made possible by those who went before him. They are the people whose stories are included in this biography and history series, as well as thousands of others who remain nameless. They are people who depend upon you to carry on the dream of liberty and justice for all people of the world.

Civil Rights Movement Time Line

1954

May 17—
Brown v. Board of Education of Topeka I: Supreme Court rules racial segregation in public is unconstitutional.

1955

May 31—
Brown v. Board of Education of Topeka II: Supreme Court says desegregation of public schools must proceed "with all deliberate speed."

August 28—
14-year-old Emmett Till is killed in Money, Mississippi.

December 5, 1955–December 20, 1956—
Montgomery, Alabama bus boycott.

1956

November 13—
Supreme Court outlaws racial segregation on Alabama's city buses.

1957

January 10, 11—
Southern Christian Leadership Conference (SCLC) is founded.

August 29—
Civil Rights Act is passed. Among other things, it creates Civil Rights Commission to advise the president and gives government power to uphold voting rights.

September 1957–
Little Rock Central High School is desegregated.

1962

September 29—
Federal troops help integrate University of Mississippi ("Ole Miss") after two people are killed and several are injured.

1963

April to May—
Birmingham, Alabama, demonstrations. School children join the marches.

May 20—
Supreme Court rules Birmingham's segregation laws are unconstitutional.

June 12—
NAACP worker Medgar Evers is killed in Jackson, Mississippi.

August 28—
March on Washington draws more than 250,000 people.

September 15—
Four girls are killed when a Birmingham church is bombed.

November 22—
President John F. Kennedy is killed in Dallas, Texas.

1964

March–June—
St. Augustine, Florida, demonstrations.

June 21—
James Chaney, Michael Schwerner, and Andrew Goodman are killed while registering black voters in Mississippi.

July 2—
Civil Rights Act is passed. Among other things, it provides for equal job opportunities and gives the government power to sue to desegregate public schools and facilities.

August—
Mississippi Freedom Democratic Party (MFDP) attempts to represent Mississippi at the Democratic National Convention.

1958 — 1959 — 1960 — 1961

September 1958–August 1959—
Little Rock Central High School is closed because governor refuses to integrate it.

February 1—
Student sit-ins at lunch counter in Greensboro, North Carolina, begin sit-in protests all over the South.

April 17—
Student Nonviolent Coordinating Committee (SNCC) is founded.

May 6—
Civil Rights Act is passed. Among other things, it allows judges to appoint people to help blacks register to vote.

Eleven African countries win their independence.

May 4—
Freedom Rides leave Washington, D.C., and head south.

September 22—
Interstate Commerce Commission ordered to enforce desegregation laws on buses, and trains, and in travel facilities like waiting rooms, rest rooms, and restaurants.

1965 — 1966 — 1967 — 1968

January–March—
Selma, Alabama, demonstrations.

February 21—
Malcolm X is killed in New York City.

March 21–25—
More than 25,000 march from Selma to Montgomery, Alabama.

August 6—
Voting Rights Act passed.

August 11–16—
Watts riot (Los Angeles, California).

June—
James Meredith "March Against Fear" from Memphis, Tennessee, to Jackson, Mississippi. Stokely Carmichael makes slogan "Black Power" famous during march.

Fall—
Black Panther Party for Self-Defense is formed by Huey Newton and Bobby Seale in Oakland, California.

June 13—
Thurgood Marshall is appointed first African-American U.S. Supreme Court justice.

Summer—
Riots break out in 30 U.S. cities.

April 4—
Martin Luther King, Jr., is killed in Memphis, Tennessee.

April 11—
Civil Rights Act is passed. Among other things, it prohibits discrimination in selling and renting houses or apartments.

May 13–June 23—
Poor People's March: Washington, D.C., to protest poverty.

"I want young men and young women who are not alive today but who will come into this world, with privileges and new opportunities. I want them to know and see that these new privileges and opportunities did not come without somebody suffering and sacrificing for them."

Martin Luther King, Jr.

1 YOU'RE AS GOOD AS ANYONE

"This is the ultimate tragedy of segregation. It not only harms one physically but injures one spiritually. It scars the soul and degrades the personality. It inflicts the segregated with a false sense of inferiority, while [giving] the segregator... a false estimate of his own superiority."

MARTIN LUTHER KING, JR.

When Martin Luther King, Jr., was born, the doctor had to spank him several times before he cried and breathed in life. But after that, his father said, he never shut up. He talked all the time. Little did his parents know that one day their son's words would influence the entire world.

Martin Luther King, Jr., was Martin Luther and Alberta King's first son, and he was named after his father. Everyone called Martin's father Mike or Daddy King, and they called

Martin Luther King, Jr. (front row right), as a child with his family.

young Martin M.L. When he was born, on January 15, 1929, M.L. already had a sister, Willie Christine, who was a year older than he was. Within another year he also had a brother, Alfred Daniel, who was called A.D. for short.

All of the King children were born at home, a two-story

Victorian frame house with a porch that went all the way around one side. It was a big house—12 rooms—but the Kings were a big family. Seven people lived there: M.L. and his sister and brother, his parents, and his Grandfather and Grandmother Williams.

M.L.'s family lived on Sweet Auburn, as they called their street. Auburn Avenue was in a prosperous African-American section of Atlanta, Georgia. That part of town contained some of the largest black-owned businesses in the United States. On Auburn Avenue there were two insurance companies, and a drugstore that became part of a chain of five throughout the city. Most of the people who lived in that neighborhood were fairly well off. They were teachers, lawyers, dentists, doctors, ministers, and businesspeople.

M.L.'s family wasn't wealthy, but they weren't poor either. Their home was comfortable, and there was always plenty of food. The children had good clothes, nice toys, and music lessons. The family even owned a car. Daddy King and his father-in-law, the Reverend Adam Daniel Williams, were pastors of the Ebenezer Baptist Church. It was a prosperous church, so its pastors were well paid.

Ebenezer was only a few blocks from M.L.'s home. It was a second home to him. His mother played the organ there. Members of the church fussed over him just the way his family did. Church played a big part in M.L.'s life. Every day at the King house began and ended with family prayer. At their evening meals, the children recited passages they had memorized from the Bible. After dinner, Grandmother Williams thrilled them with exciting stories from the Bible.

Young M.L. spent his days riding the bike he shared with A.D. or flying kites and model airplanes. He also liked to roller-skate with Christine on the sidewalk in front of the house. At other times he played baseball with the neighborhood children in an open field behind the King home. M.L. played hard to make up for being small for his age. He was always out to prove that he was as strong and scrappy as the bigger children.

By the time he was five, M.L. could recite long passages from the Bible. And he loved books. Daddy King said that even before his son could read, he just liked to have books around him. One day M.L. told his mother, "Just you wait and see. When I grow up I'm going to get me some big words."

M.L. was so smart that his mother decided to slip him into school a year early along with Christine. M.L. was smart enough to keep up with the other children, but, as his daddy said, he couldn't keep his mouth shut. One day he told everyone in the class about his latest birthday party. As he was proudly describing the five candles on his birthday cake, his teachers overheard him and sent him home to wait another year.

M.L. entered the first grade again—this time when he was supposed to. One afternoon after school he ran across the street to tell his best playmate all about his day. His friend's parents owned a store across from the King home. He and M.L. had always played together until that fall, when they began attending separate schools. Ever since school began, his friend's mother wouldn't let her son see M.L. Today she told him why. It was because her boy was white and M.L. was "colored."

Colored was a term used for blacks, or African Americans. Other terms have also been used throughout the years, such as

Negro, *Afro-American*, and *people of color*. Depending upon how a term was used, it could be insulting or reflect pride. This time the term *colored* was not used respectfully. M.L.'s friend's mother meant that M.L. wasn't good enough to play with her son because M.L. wasn't white.

M.L. was stunned. He had never thought about his white friend being different. He hadn't even thought much about their going to different schools when they both entered the first grade. Hurt and confused, M.L. rushed home crying to find out why this had happened.

That evening his parents told M.L. about the "race problem." He learned what it meant to be "colored" in the United States, especially in the Deep South where they lived. His parents told him all about slavery. It had begun hundreds of years ago, when Africans were kidnapped and brought to this country to be slaves.

At that time, people owned slaves just as they owned land or horses. They used slaves to do their work for them. Owners could treat their slaves any way they wanted to treat them, and the slaves had to do whatever their owners told them to do. Slaves—even children—could be sold and sent far away from their families.

After the Civil War was fought, slavery ended. However, whites still kept their power over blacks with Jim Crow laws. Jim Crow was the name given to a system that kept blacks separate from whites. This system of separation was also called segregation. One of these Jim Crow laws said that Martin and his white friend had to attend separate schools. M.L.'s school was an all-black school. His friend's school was an all-white school.

Segregation was used to keep blacks from bettering themselves. There were many well-paying jobs that African Americans simply weren't allowed to have. Because of segregation, it was difficult for African Americans to become doctors, lawyers, dentists, or teachers. Whites everywhere could attend schools that allowed them to prepare for these professions, but few of these schools were open to blacks.

Mr. and Mrs. King told M.L. about some of the terrible wrongs they had seen done to black people. They recalled insults they themselves had received from white people just because they were black. When M.L. heard this, he was shocked. Why did white people hate him so much? Right then he decided to hate all white people since they hated him so much. What was wrong with him, anyway? he wondered. But his mother told him that he must never feel that he was less than anybody else. He must always feel that he was somebody. "You are as good as anyone," she said.

M.L. tried to remember what his mother told him—"you are as good as anyone." But every day now he began to see for himself what his parents had explained to him about racial prejudice. Soon he was able to read signs that said Whites Only or Colored. These signs were everywhere in Atlanta—in front of barbershops, restaurants, swimming pools, and playgrounds. M.L. and his family weren't allowed to enter places that were marked Whites Only. When they went to a train or bus station, they had to be careful about which door they used and which waiting room they sat in. If blacks sat down in the wrong section, they were arrested for breaking the segregation law.

Anything marked Colored was often dirty or didn't work properly. For example, M.L. could use only drinking fountains that were labeled Colored, but these were usually out of order. Even so, he couldn't take one sip from the white fountain. If Daddy King took M.L to a soda fountain for ice cream, he had to buy it at a side window. Then they had to stand outside and eat out of a paper cup instead of sitting down at tables and eating from a real dish as the whites did. This was because blacks weren't allowed to sit at lunch counters in the downtown area of Atlanta.

In places where they were allowed, blacks usually had to enter through the back door. They had to use the back doors of office buildings, then ride on freight elevators. They also had to use the back door on city buses. First they paid their fare at the front, then they got off the bus and went to the back door to enter. Sometimes the driver would drive off just for fun while they were walking to the back. Once they were inside, blacks could sit only in the back of the bus. If there were no more seats left, they were forced to stand while the whites sat in their seats.

The first time M.L. went to a movie, he discovered that he had to enter by a special side door. Then he found himself sitting on lumpy seats in the back balcony that was set aside for blacks. It was difficult to see or hear the movie from there. No one ever cleaned this section. The floor was covered with old popcorn and was sticky from spilled drinks. Down below him, the whites sat in clean, comfortable seats.

M.L. began to see that many white people really thought they were superior to blacks. They still felt that blacks were their servants and should act like slaves all the time. He noticed that if blacks didn't behave the way whites thought they should—even if this happened accidentally—the whites often became violently angry. One day he was shopping with his mother in a downtown Atlanta store. Suddenly a white woman ran up to him, slapped him, and screamed, "That little nigger stepped on my foot!" Not even his mother could save him from these surprise attacks.

M.L. found out for himself how badly Jim Crow laws hurt black people in employment. When he was eight years old he got a newspaper route for the *Atlanta Journal*. By the time he was 13, M.L. had become the youngest assistant manager of a delivery station. But that was as far as he could go. No matter how hard he worked or how well he did his job, he could never become the station manager. M.L. was black, and only whites became managers.

The more signs of white hatred M.L. saw, the more he hated whites. His parents told him to love whites. It was his Christian duty, his father said. But M.L. asked Daddy King, "How can I love people who hate me?"

2 THE LONG BATTLE

"Freedom is never given to anybody. For the oppressor has you in domination because he wants to keep you there."

MARTIN LUTHER KING, JR.

Young M.L. came from a family whose members fought to change the system of segregation that oppressed them. His grandfather, the Reverend Adam Daniel Williams, was born the son of a slave preacher. After Dr. Williams became the pastor of the Ebenezer Baptist Church in 1894, he made it one of the most important African-American churches in Atlanta.

Dr. Williams was active in fighting for the rights of African Americans. He was the first president of the Atlanta chapter of the National Association for the Advancement of Colored People (NAACP) shortly after it was founded in 1909. The NAACP was the first national organization to become concerned with issues that affected African Americans.

At the time Dr. Williams joined the NAACP, it was dangerous to do so—especially in the South. Racial prejudice existed in the North as well as in the South, but conditions there weren't as bad as they were in the South. Many southern whites felt that any blacks who talked about their rights were getting "uppity" and didn't know their place. They felt that these blacks should be taught how to act properly. "Uppity niggers" and white "nigger lovers" ran the risk of having their homes burned by whites. They also risked being lynched.

At this time lynching black men, women, and children was a common practice in the South. In these lynchings, blacks were grabbed by gangs of angry whites and killed. They were usually tortured first, then hanged from a tree or shot. But they were never given a trial to determine whether they were guilty or innocent of whatever crime they had been accused of committing. Usually the victims of these lynchings had done or said something that blacks weren't supposed to do or say to whites. Often a black man was wrongly accused of raping a white woman. This could happen if a black man was simply walking down the street and a white woman looked at him.

The Ku Klux Klan was an organization of whites who were especially violent toward blacks. The Ku Klux Klan believed in white supremacy—that white people were better than any other race. They met secretly and wore white robes with pointed hoods that covered their faces. At night these ghostlike figures thundered through the black sections of a town on horses, carrying torches and firing guns. Sometimes the Klan burned a cross on someone's lawn. Sometimes they burned black people.

Many people besides the Ku Klux Klan didn't believe blacks had any rights. These people simply didn't think of blacks as human beings. Whites who had too much honor to cheat another white person saw no dishonor in cheating blacks. Taking property away from blacks wasn't really stealing to them. Killing a black person—even a child—wasn't murder to them.

Dr. Williams railed against this attitude in whites. When a white newspaper in Atlanta called blacks "dirty and ignorant," he helped to lead a boycott of that paper. A boycott is a form of protest in which a large group of people refuse to buy or use something. As a result, the business loses money. Eventually the Atlanta boycott caused the paper to close down.

Like Dr. Williams, Daddy King also came from a poor family. Born in 1899, he was one of 10 children raised on a sharecropping farm in Georgia. Being a sharecropper wasn't very different from being a slave. When the slaves were given their freedom after the Civil War, they had nothing with which to start a new life. They no longer had a home on the plantation where they had spent their entire lives. Many of them turned to the only work they knew how to do—working in the fields. Since they had no money with which to buy or rent land, they often farmed part of their former owner's land. For rent, grain, and other supplies they needed to farm, they gave the owner half of their crops.

To start out, the black families had to borrow money from the owner in order to buy the food they would need until their crops were harvested. When it was time to pay their debts, the sharecroppers usually were told that they owed their landlord just about what their share of the crop was worth. This meant that they often had to give the landlord all of the crops they had grown and borrow all over again in order to live through the year.

Young Mike plowed the fields on his parents' farm with a mule. When he was 16 years old, he went to Atlanta. There he "felt the call" from God to become a Baptist minister. Soon he was pastoring two small churches. Then he met and fell in love with Alberta Williams, Dr. Williams's daughter. They were worlds apart. She was attending Spelman College, an elite, all-black women's college in Atlanta. Mike was attending classes to earn his high-school diploma.

Alberta had lived a comfortable and sheltered life. Mike had experienced the harsh side of life, where poverty sometimes made people mean. She was shy, gentle, thoughtful, and well-mannered. He was bold, rough, quick-tempered, and outspoken. The two young people didn't mind these differences, but Alberta's father did. Mike would have to better himself with more education if he wanted to win Dr. Williams's approval.

Mike courted Alberta for six years while he worked on his high-school diploma. When he enrolled in Morehouse College, an all-black college in Atlanta, Dr. Williams finally gave his approval. On Thanksgiving Day in 1926, Mike and Alberta married and moved into her parents' home on Auburn Avenue.

Soon King became the assistant pastor at the Ebenezer Baptist Church. When Dr. Williams died suddenly of a stroke in 1931, King became the new pastor. Over the next few years, he renovated Ebenezer and raised its membership from 600 to several thousand members and six choirs. The church prospered, and so did Mike King.

Daddy King was able to provide for his family during the Great Depression, which struck in 1929, the year M.L. was born. During the Great Depression banks went broke, and many people lost all the money they had saved. They also lost their jobs and had to go on welfare, which meant accepting small sums of money and food from the government.

Churches set up soup kitchens to feed as many as they could. As he grew up, M.L. saw out-of-work people standing in line for a meal. Often these breadlines stretched around city blocks. M.L. was worried that these poor people wouldn't be able to feed their children.

The Great Depression lasted through the 1930s. But Daddy King's children not only had all the food and clothing they needed, but also weekly allowances for treats. He was determined that his children wouldn't suffer as he had when he was growing up.

To M.L., Daddy King was always "straightening out" the white people. One day Daddy King was taking M.L. some-

Millions stood in line for food at soup kitchens during the depression.

where in the family car when a police officer told him to pull over. The officer leaned in the window and said to Daddy King, "Boy, let me see your license."

Daddy King pointed to M.L. and replied, "This is a boy. I'm a man; and until you call me one, I will not listen to you."

Another time Daddy King took M.L. to buy new shoes. In the store the clerk told them, "I'll be happy to wait on you if you'll just move to those seats in the rear."

"There's nothing wrong with these seats," said Daddy King firmly.

Then the clerk said, "Sorry, but you'll have to move."

"We'll either buy shoes sitting here," replied Daddy King, "or we won't buy shoes at all!" With that he and M.L. got up and walked out of the store.

Daddy King was active in the NAACP and had led Atlanta blacks in a voting rights march in 1936. He told M.L. and all of his children, "Nobody can make a slave out of you if you don't think like a slave." But however strongly he supported his children's right to be free outside of his house, inside he was the ruler. He felt he knew what was best for his family. His word was law and he didn't tolerate any other point of view—not even from Alberta or Grandmother Williams.

The children didn't dare disagree with their father. When they broke a rule or talked back, Daddy King took out the strap and gave them a harsh whipping. Daddy King's whippings made M.L. very angry, but he never cried out. He just stood silently while he was being strapped, tears running down his face.

When the whippings were over, M.L. would run to Grandmother Williams for comfort. It upset her so much when M.L. was whipped that she'd burst into tears and run into another room. It was this special tenderness Grandmother Williams felt for M.L. that made her the person he loved most. M.L. felt so close to his grandmother that he called her Mama. He loved his mother, too, but she wasn't as warm and affectionate as Mama

Highlights in the Life of Martin Luther King, Jr.

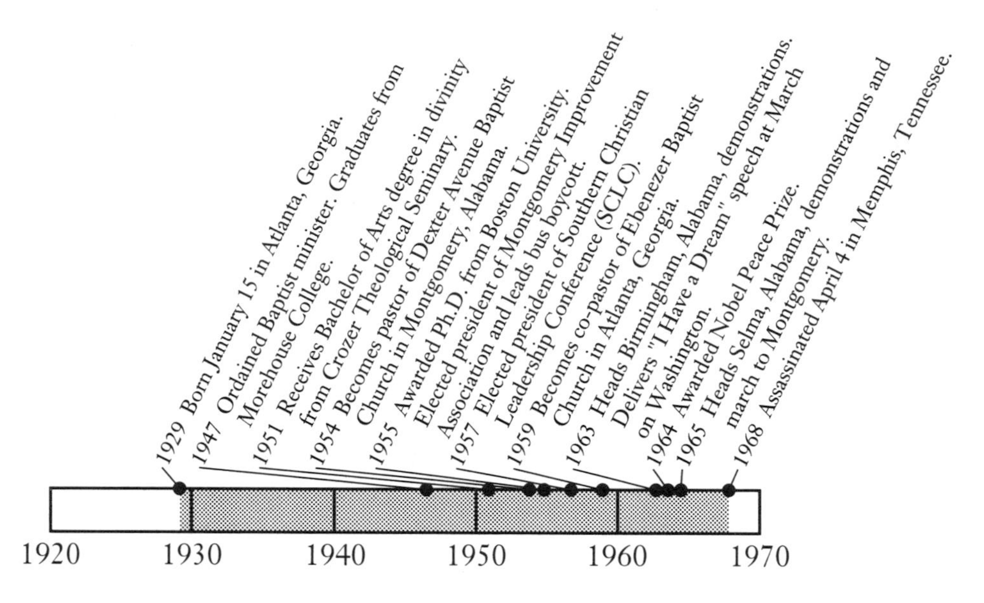

was. Alberta was so formal that her children called her Mother Dear. All of Mama's grandchildren felt something special for her, but everyone knew that M.L. was her favorite.

Even after Dr. Williams died, Mama kept up her church activities. One Sunday afternoon in May, she went off to speak at a church event. That afternoon, 12-year-old M.L. slipped out to watch a parade—even though he was supposed to be at home studying. He was having a great time when one of his friends found him and delivered the worst news possible. Mama was dead.

Grandmother Williams had died of a heart attack at the church where she was to speak. M.L. was sure that God was punishing his family because he had sinned that day. If he hadn't gone to the parade, Mama would still be alive. No one could convince him that it wasn't his fault that the most important person in his life was dead. For days he had long crying spells and couldn't sleep.

He was miserable without Mama. Nothing would ever be the same for him. No one in his life was as warm and loving as she had been. Who could he run to for comfort now when Daddy King whipped him? Who would hug him?

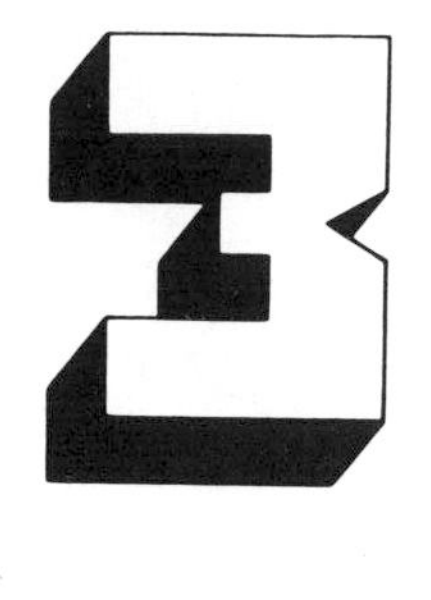

THE JOURNEY

"Whatever career you may choose for yourself [also] become a dedicated fighter for civil rights.... It will make you a better doctor, a better lawyer, a better teacher. ... Make a career of humanity. ... You will make a greater person of yourself, a greater nation of your country, and a finer world to live in."

MARTIN LUTHER KING, JR.

After Mama died, M.L. began to have doubts about his religion. He believed in the Christian idea of life after death because he felt that somehow his grandmother still lived. But he no longer believed many of the Bible stories that Mama had told him. One week in Sunday school, he said that he didn't believe Christ's body had risen from the dead. This kind of talk, coming from Rev. Martin Luther King's son, shocked the Sunday school teacher. M.L. began to question other beliefs of the Bible and those of his Baptist religion.

He also felt uncomfortable with all the displays of emotion he had to sit through during church services at Ebenezer. Each Sunday his father worked up the congregation until people cried and clapped and sang. People shouted in answer to Daddy King as he preached. Soon there was a certain rhythm going, as if King and the congregation were singing the words of a song. The minister called out a sentence, and the members answered, "Amen, Brother" or "That's right" or "Hallelujah." They stood up and swayed back and forth, feeling the spirit of the Lord. M.L. didn't think this kind of behavior was very respectable. It embarrassed him to watch his father act this way.

M.L. began to wonder whether religion really did anyone any good. He especially didn't think Daddy King's kind of religion had any meaning to people anymore. His father expected him to follow in the footsteps of the men in his family, but M.L. didn't want to be a preacher. When he told his father that he had other ideas, Daddy King was very upset with him.

M.L. didn't know what he wanted to be, but his world now centered around Booker T. Washington High School—the all-black high school Grandfather Williams had helped to establish. Maybe his textbooks would give him some of the answers he was seeking.

One of M.L.'s favorite subjects was history. He began to learn about African-American men and women who had made history in the United States. He read about Frederick Douglass, who was born a slave but escaped to become a great and fiery speaker. Douglass traveled around the country telling people what it was like to be a slave. He was also an abolitionist—that is, someone who wanted to end, or abolish, slavery.

M.L. also read about Harriet Tubman, another escaped slave. She helped to set up escape routes from the South to the North for other runaway slaves. Her famous escape system was part of what was called the Underground Railroad. As M.L. read about African Americans who had done so much to better the world, he knew that someday he wanted to do his part, too. But how?

M.L.'s other favorite subject was English. He studied the great writers and speakers. He loved the way they put big words together. M.L. was already "getting himself some big words," just as he had said he would when he was a child. In the 11th grade he entered an oratorical, or speaking, contest in Dublin, Georgia, 90 miles from Atlanta. One of his favorite teachers, Sarah Grace Bradley, went with him on the bus trip.

M.L. had written a speech to recite entitled "The Negro and the Constitution." He hoped it was good enough to win a prize. There was something else he wanted to test as well. During the past year, M.L.'s voice had changed. It had deepened into a rich, low baritone. He began to notice that whenever he spoke, the sound of his voice alone made people listen to him.

The judges awarded M.L. a prize for his speech. Afterward, he and Mrs. Bradley proudly boarded a crowded bus to return to Atlanta. The two of them were talking about the exciting day when the bus stopped to pick up more passengers. There were no more empty seats. Since these new passengers were white, the bus driver walked to the back of the bus to tell blacks who were sitting that they would have to give up their seats.

The driver stopped beside M.L. and Mrs. Bradley and ordered them to get up. When they didn't move quickly enough he began cursing them, calling them "black sons of bitches." M.L. became so angry that he decided to stay right in his seat. But Mrs. Bradley urged him to get up, saying they had to obey the law. They stood in the aisle for the full 90-mile trip home.

The bus sped along, lurching from side to side, while M.L. fumed and struggled to keep his balance. All his pride had been turned to humiliation and rage. He had just delivered a speech that showed how the U.S. Constitution affected African Americans. But the bus driver had just reminded him that the Constitution didn't really apply equally to his people after all. He hated white people more than ever now. M.L. never forgot that night. "That night will never leave my mind," he said later. "It was the angriest I have ever been in my life."

M.L. felt anger toward whites, and he often felt anger toward

his father. Neither white people nor Daddy King would give him much independence. Along with the anger, M.L. had a mixture of feelings for Daddy King. He admired his father a great deal, but he was also afraid of him. Sometimes M.L. didn't know what to make of all these feelings. He respected his father, but it embarrassed him and made him angry when his father whipped him. It also frustrated him when his father rejected his opinions.

As M.L. moved into his teenage years, his need for independence from his father grew stronger. He tried to avoid conflicts with Daddy King because they almost always ended with a whipping. He could hardly bear it that his father was still whipping him when he was 15 years old. Some of the anger he felt toward his father was turned into energy when he played sports. He was so fierce that his friends couldn't tell whether he was playing or fighting.

But M.L. didn't like to fight. He preferred to talk and try to work out some solution to a disagreement. If talk failed, he wasn't afraid to throw a few punches. "Let's go to the grass," he'd say, but only if he had no choice. Fighting made him feel bad inside, he said.

During his high-school years, M.L. took violin lessons and developed a liking for opera. His fondness for snazzy clothes, especially tweed suits, earned him the nickname Tweedie. He also developed another interest—girls. He discovered that they, too, responded to his rich, deep voice and to his big words. They blushed and giggled when he started his smooth talking. M.L. had so many girlfriends that his brother, A.D., couldn't keep up with him.

In spite of his many interests, M.L. did so well in school that he skipped two grades. He was only 15 years old when he enrolled in Morehouse College in 1944. To help pay for some of his college expenses, Morehouse arranged a summer job for M.L. on a tobacco farm in Connecticut. This was his first time away from home. The work was hard. But in spite of long, hot hours in the strong-smelling tobacco fields and smoke houses, M.L. loved it up north.

On the weekends he and his friends went into the nearby city of Hartford. Here he discovered what it was like to live somewhere other than in the South. In Hartford he not only could eat in any restaurant, he could also sit wherever he wanted to sit. He could go into any motion-picture theater—through the front door—and sit in the front row. The sense of freedom he felt was thrilling.

At the end of the summer, M.L. took a train back to Atlanta. As the train reached Virginia, he made his way to the dining car. When he started to sit down, the waiter quickly led him to a table at the back of the car. Then he pulled a curtain down in front of M.L. to hide him from the white passengers. M.L. was in the South again, where just the sight of him was offensive to whites. Later he said that as he sat there staring at the curtain, he felt "as though the curtain had been dropped on my selfhood."

Incidents like these made M.L. more determined to do something to change the way blacks in this country had to live. But how? Maybe the best way was to become a lawyer. His mother suggested that he become a doctor, but he didn't think that was the profession for him. That year he "had the calling" to be a minister. In other words, he began to feel that God had put him on earth for that purpose. But M.L. tried to ignore those feelings. There was one thing he knew for sure, however: He wasn't going to be a preacher.

A NEW KIND OF PREACHER

"Any religion that professes to be concerned with the souls of men and is not concerned with the slums that damn them, the economic conditions that strangle them, and the social conditions that cripple them is a dry-as-dust religion."

MARTIN LUTHER KING, JR.

When M.L. entered Morehouse College, he knew that he wanted to help African Americans, but he didn't know exactly how he would go about this. He decided to take sociology—the study of the development and behavior of people. He felt this subject would give him a better understanding of people. Because of his love of big words, he also studied English in order to become a better speaker.

M.L. had always gotten good grades, but at Morehouse he suddenly began to have difficulty with his studies. He was shocked to discover that he could read only as well as an eighth grader. A professor at Morehouse explained that even though M.L. had gotten good grades, he hadn't received the best education. This was because the all-black public schools M.L. had been forced to attend weren't as good as the all-white public schools. The school boards didn't think it was important for African Americans to have a good education. As a result, black schools didn't receive the same amount of money that was given to white schools. This showed in their equipment and books, which weren't as good as those found in the all-white schools. In addition, the quality of the education black teachers themselves had received wasn't equal to that of white teachers. This sometimes affected their teaching ability.

M.L. felt cheated and bitter. This was even more reason to hate white people and segregation. He had to do extra work on top of his regular studies to catch up with his classmates. By his second year, however, he had begun to get straight A's again in his English, history, sociology, and philosophy classes.

Several teachers at Morehouse College inspired young M.L. His English professor, Gladstone Chandler, taught his students by playing word games in class. Whenever Chandler asked his students a question, he expected them to answer using new words they had learned. Instead of "thinking," for example, M.L. would "cogitate." Or he was "quiescent" rather than "resting." M.L. was really "getting some big words" now.

But it was Dr. Benjamin Mays, the president of the college, who most influenced M.L. during his term at Morehouse. Dr. Mays told his students that "a man should do his job so well that the living, the dead, and the unborn could do it no better." He believed it was education that would set African Americans free. He was active in the NAACP and spoke out against racial prejudice—unlike many educators, who were afraid that this kind of activity would cost them their jobs.

Dr. Mays felt that the church should be more involved with improving the lives and communities of African Americans. Most African-American preachers told their congregations not to worry about the terrible conditions of this life. They promised that their people would find peace, freedom, and equality in their next life in heaven. Listening to Dr. Mays and other professors made M.L. rethink his attitude about religion and the church.

M.L. had nearly rejected religion, especially his father's religion, after Mama died. Daddy King believed that if the Bible said something was so, that was that. M.L. had a difficult time accepting this idea, as well as Daddy King's emotional way of preaching. He struggled over what the role of the church should be to the people who went there for guidance and strength. His questioning had forced him to think deeply about what he believed and what the church should do. At Morehouse, he found people who, unlike his father, were eager to discuss these questions. Discussing different ideas at Morehouse helped M.L. to sort out his own beliefs.

The professors at Morehouse also encouraged their students to discuss racial problems, such as segregation, and to look for solutions. The Supreme Court itself had made segregation legal in 1896 with a court case called *Plessy* v. *Ferguson*. This case came to be known as the "separate but equal" case. It made separation of blacks from whites legal as long as blacks were given equal public facilities such as schools, hospitals, and rest rooms.

One problem with this law was that blacks found it insulting to be kept apart from everyone else. Separation made them feel as if they weren't worthy of being with other people. Another problem with this policy was that the separate facilities that had been set aside for blacks were rarely equal to those used by whites. They were usually of poorer quality than the facilities for whites. These lower standards often kept blacks from improving their own conditions. M.L. had learned firsthand how inferior black schools had affected the quality of his own education.

In an attempt to find solutions to these problems, M.L. studied black history and read the writings of important black

Booker T. Washington, shown during his term as president of Tuskegee Institute.

thinkers. Around 1896, when *Plessy* v. *Ferguson* was ruled on, Booker T. Washington, a noted African-American leader and educator, was advising blacks to accept segregation. He told blacks to forget about fighting for equality with whites and just learn a skill or trade. Washington started the Tuskegee Institute in Alabama. Tuskegee was an important black college where thousands of black people were trained in such practical trades as carpentry, farming, and mechanics. Washington felt that if blacks stayed separate and imitated whites, they would be more acceptable to whites and therefore be left to live in peace.

But Washington was wrong about blacks being left in peace. After the Civil War ended slavery, lynchings and riots against blacks became more and more common. As slaves, African

Americans had actually been safer than they were after they were freed. A slave owner would rarely kill a valuable worker, especially one who didn't have to be paid. But free blacks had to have wages. They even opened up their own businesses and began to compete with whites. In order to frighten blacks and keep them in their place, the number of lynchings increased. To fight against this violence, W.E.B. Du Bois, a scholar and proud black leader, helped to found the NAACP in 1909. Other goals of the NAACP were to achieve "equal citizenship rights for all American citizens by eliminating segregation and discrimination in housing, employment, voting, schools, the courts, transportation, [and] recreation."

Author W.E.B. Du Bois was a scholar who helped foster African-American pride.

M.L. learned that Du Bois did not believe in voluntary segregation. Instead, he felt that African Americans should fight for integration. He also felt that the kind of training Washington favored would limit the leadership qualities of some African Americans. Du Bois thought that talented African Americans should have opportunities for higher education. However, much later in his life, Du Bois became bitter over how difficult it was for blacks to achieve progress toward freedom and equality. He finally decided that it was better for blacks to live separately from whites.

M.L. read about another African-American leader who thought that blacks should separate themselves from whites. Marcus Garvey, the founder of the Universal Negro Improvement Association, started a back to Africa movement during the early 1900s. Garvey urged African Americans to return to the home of their ancestors.

M.L. didn't agree with any of these attitudes. He believed that if African Americans accepted segregation, their minds and souls would remain enslaved. He also thought it was a bad idea for African Americans to return to Africa. Most of them had been living in the United States for many years, and Africa would be a strange place to them. M.L. felt that the United States was their home, so African Americans should try to make it a better place for themselves.

Dr. Mays showed M.L. how a minister could improve conditions for African Americans. A minister could do something about issues that affected his congregation—issues such as hunger, poverty, and prejudice. He also showed M.L. that he didn't have to be the same kind of preacher his father was. He could use reason as well as emotion in his sermons to lead his people.

Largely because of Dr. Mays, when M.L. was 17 he decided to become a minister. When he told his father of his decision, Daddy King couldn't have been happier. But he wouldn't allow M.L to see his pleasure. Instead, Daddy King sternly told his son that he would have to prove himself by preaching a trial sermon. If he preached well, that would be a sign that this was what he really wanted to do with his life.

Because it was a trial sermon, M.L. would speak from one of the small chapels in the church basement. That Sunday, however, so many people crowded into the basement that everyone had to move upstairs to the main chapel. M.L. knew that everyone was curious to see how well Rev. King's boy would do. Many remembered how he had questioned the Bible only a few years earlier. He felt very nervous standing before his father and a full house. Finally he took heart, grabbed the pulpit with both hands, and began to speak.

To everyone's joy, M.L.'s sermon was a roaring success. The next year, 1948, he was ordained a minister and made the assistant pastor at the Ebenezer Baptist Church. He was only 18, but somehow he seemed older and wiser than his years. He had also shed his youthful nickname of M.L. Now he was called Martin.

Martin was now a co-pastor at Ebenezer, with adult responsibilities. Nevertheless, Daddy King still saw himself as the rule maker both at home and at church. When he found out that Martin had been out dancing one night, he made his son apologize to the congregation the next Sunday. Dancing was a sin, according to Daddy King.

Rev. King also didn't like it when Martin went to work that summer as a laborer for a white business in Atlanta. Daddy King didn't want white bosses degrading his son. But Martin wanted to know what it was like to work for whites. He took a job unloading goods from trucks and train cars for the Railway Express Company. He quit the first time the boss called him a "nigger." Then he took a similar job at the Southern Spring and Mattress Company. There he learned that blacks earned less than whites did, even though they did the same work. Daddy King was right. Working for whites could make a black person feel degraded.

Martin stood up to his father again when he joined a new club, the Atlanta Intercollegiate Council. The group was made up of students from Atlanta's black and white colleges. Daddy King told Martin that he should stay with his own kind. The white students couldn't be trusted, he said. Martin may have disliked whites, but he didn't think this kind of thinking made any sense.

As he spent more and more time with whites, Martin began to hate them less and less. He got to know each person as an individual, not just as part of a group. As he got to know the white people in this club, his anger softened. He began to see that they weren't the enemy. The enemy was segregation. Martin felt that segregation kept people from understanding each other and caused fear and suspicion.

After a while, Martin found that he didn't even hate the white people he worked for that summer. To him, the problem between the different races was caused by the economic system. In order to make more money, employers tried to pay as little as they could in wages and often cheated their employees. The employees who were cheated the most were the ones who had the fewest rights and could make the fewest demands. These were the blacks.

How could Martin change society? How could he become a different kind of preacher? How could he help African Americans win more rights so they could do better in the economic system? An essay written in 1849 by Henry David Thoreau gave him an answer.

Thoreau was a white writer who had lived about 100 years earlier. His essay, called "Civil Disobedience," was about a certain kind of protesting. It said that if someone believed a law wasn't just, he or she had the right to disobey it. Of course, this person also had to be willing to go to jail for breaking the law.

Thoreau had refused to pay his taxes as a protest against slavery and was put into jail for his actions. When a friend visited him and asked him why he was in jail, Thoreau answered, "Why are you out of jail?" This kind of thinking and action inspired Martin.

When Martin graduated from Morehouse College in the spring of 1948, many different philosophies were milling around in his head. He had earned a degree in sociology. Now he wanted another degree in divinity, the study of religious beliefs and practices. He had decided to attend Crozer Seminary in Chester, Pennsylvania.

Crozer was one of the best seminaries in the United States. It was also integrated, and it was out of the South. Martin had had a taste of freedom from segregation when he worked in the tobacco fields of Connecticut and spent his weekends in Hartford. He wanted to go north again. He had also experienced the freedom of discussing ideas with an open mind, and he wanted to attend a school that would allow him to do just that. Furthermore, he wanted to get away from his father. He needed to find his own way. Crozer would allow him to enjoy all these freedoms.

Daddy King had assumed that his son would marry a young woman he had been dating and settle down to a life of preaching at Ebenezer. But Martin wasn't ready to get married. He was only 19, and he wanted to be on his own. In the fall of 1948, he set out for Crozer. He hoped to find answers to the big questions he had about himself and what he could do to help the world.

5 PIECES OF A PUZZLE

"[People] often hate each other because they fear each other; they fear each other because they do not know each other; they do not know each other because they cannot communicate; they cannot communicate because they are separated."

MARTIN LUTHER KING, JR.

Crozer Theological Seminary was a small private school near Philadelphia. It was truly integrated. Martin had Chinese, Japanese, Indian, black, and white classmates, both men and women. Martin had never gone to school with whites before, and he felt as if they were always watching him. He knew that many whites thought that blacks were lazy, unclean, always out for a good time, and always late. For this reason, he was determined to look and act just the opposite. He wore suits and ties. His room was spotless, and his shoes were always shined. He was "grimly serious," as he put it, and, "if I were a minute late to class I was... sure everyone noticed it."

Martin was so concerned with being a perfect black student that he didn't take time to get to know the other students.

One night as he sat reading, a white student from North Carolina burst into his room. The student accused Martin of pulling a room raid. This was a prank students often played on one another—sneaking into someone's room and messing it up. Martin tried to explain that he'd been in his room all evening reading and that it must have been someone else. Before he knew what was happening, the angry student had pulled a gun and begun screaming, "You can't get away with this. Now I'm going to kill myself a darkie."

Even after he heard the insulting word "darkie," Martin remained calm. He repeated that he hadn't done anything. By this time three other students heard the shouting and had rushed to Martin's room. They forced the white student to put down his gun and reported the ugly scene to the student council.

The students who helped Martin were very angry about their classmate's actions. There was no room at Crozer for racism. But Martin wouldn't press charges against him. After a while, the young man apologized to Martin in public.

At first the other students didn't understand why Martin refused to teach this racist student a lesson. After the apology, however, they admired Martin's decision because the student now felt differently about blacks. Martin and the white student later became good friends. After that incident, Martin relaxed a bit and became more involved with school affairs.

He even took time out for fun. Crozer had a recreation room with three pool tables. The sight of pool tables in a religious college was shocking to most of the students. Many religions, including the Baptist religion, considered playing pool a sin. Martin soon decided otherwise, however, and by his second year he had become a good player. When his father visited one week, Martin boldly invited him to play the game. The older King refused and objected to his son's playing as well.

Martin told his father that a pool hall wasn't sinful. What was sinful were evil actions that might be planned there, such as a robbery. Just because people planned sinful ideas in a pool hall didn't make the pool hall itself sinful, he argued.

Daddy King wasn't convinced. He called Martin's attitude a book-learning excuse for sin. Martin gently teased his father about being old-fashioned, and his father demanded respect for his beliefs, saying they had always worked for him. Martin's sense of himself was growing stronger. He now dared to bring up a situation that he knew Daddy King would disapprove of. He was trying to find a way to discuss these conflicts with his strong, unbending father.

Martin was also trying to find a way to deal with other conflicts, such as evil in the world. Once again, he hoped to find the answers to his questions in the books he read. He studied the Bible, church history, ethics, and philosophy. The philosophy classes were his favorite. He wanted answers, and each philosopher he read had one.

One philosopher Martin studied, Walter Rauschenbusch, became a major influence on him. Rauschenbusch was a Baptist minister in one of the roughest sections of New York City during the early 1900s. His experiences had convinced him that a Christian should be involved in achieving social justice. He thought Christians could show God's love by helping society to help its people. He believed that a just society was living proof of God's love.

Rauschenbusch also believed that the economic system of capitalism as it exists in the United States created an evil society. He did not believe that people were naturally evil; they were simply the product of an evil society. This made sense to Martin. He remembered how black workers were paid less than whites by the Southern Spring and Mattress Company. Martin felt that capitalism was "always in danger of inspiring men to be more concerned about making a living than making a life."

But what system would create a better society? Martin wondered. He began studying communism but rejected it for several reasons. He rejected the Communist belief that people don't need God. He didn't think people could create a better world by themselves. He also rejected the belief that the end justifies the means. To him, no matter how worthy a goal was, it wasn't all right for a person to achieve it by doing anything he or she had to do. For Martin, if the means was unfair, hurt others, or compromised a belief, it was no good.

Martin also disagreed with the Communist idea that the government should be more important than the people who formed it. This kind of system didn't give people the freedom to think for themselves or to make choices.

In spite of his strong beliefs, however, Martin was still confused about how he could improve society. It was as if he were collecting the pieces of a puzzle and when he had put all the right pieces together, he would have the answer. He found another important piece during a lecture on India.

For many years, India had been ruled by Great Britain. In 1947, India formed its own government largely because of Mohandas Gandhi. Gandhi created a revolution there without guns, and he had gotten part of the idea from Henry David Thoreau. Gandhi taught his followers that they must disobey the unjust British laws and be ready to go to jail for doing so.

But Gandhi carried Thoreau's idea of disobeying unjust laws a step further. He organized strikes, boycotts, and protest marches on purpose so that he and his followers would be arrested. He wanted his people to fill the jails so that the world would pay attention to the terrible laws that had put them there. He taught them not to strike back or run away if their jailers beat them. Instead, they were supposed to love their enemies.

Gandhi believed that love and truth were the most powerful weapons in the world. By not fighting back, Gandhi's followers could show their enemies new ways of relating to other human beings—through love. By using love, the Indian people wouldn't defeat the British. Instead, they would change them and save them from their evil ways. Gandhi's plan worked.

Mohandas Gandhi, whose philosophy of nonviolent protest led India to freedom and inspired King.

Here was the method for changing society that Martin had been seeking. Could it work for African Americans? he wondered. There were big differences between the two countries. In India, Gandhi's people had outnumbered the British. In the United States, there were fewer blacks than whites. In addition, the feelings between the Indians and the British weren't as bitter or as deep as those between blacks and whites.

During his senior year at Crozer, Martin experienced the hatred between blacks and whites in a very new way. He fell in love with a white woman, and they even talked about getting married. But everyone the couple knew was against it. Finally, to end the relationship, the young woman's family sent her away. Martin was bitter over the fact that they had been separated only because of racial prejudice. They never had a chance to discover what their true feelings for each other were.

At about this time, Martin was reading the works of Reinhold Niebuhr, an American clergyman and philosopher. Niebuhr believed that people sinned on purpose, simply because they wanted to. Then they came up with a reason for why they "had" to do it. After the experience with his white girlfriend, Martin understood what Niebuhr meant. Well-meaning people—both black and white—had treated him and his white girlfriend cruelly. He now understood how people could convince themselves that they had good reasons for committing sins. But what could he do about it?

In June 1951, after being at Crozer for two and a half years, Martin graduated with a bachelor of arts degree in divinity. He was at the head of his class, the valedictorian, and he gave the valedictory (the farewell speech delivered at graduation ceremonies).

The next fall Martin loaded up his graduation present from Daddy King—a new green Chevrolet—and drove off to Boston. He had enrolled at Boston University School of Theology to study for a Ph.D. in theology. He had received a large scholarship to the university, where he hoped to find more pieces to his puzzle of life.

When Martin arrived at the university, he threw himself into his class work. He studied other religions and philosophies—Hinduism, Buddhism, Taoism, Confucianism, Shintoism, Judaism—as well as Christianity. Then he wrote one paper after another on the differences between these religions and their views on good and evil. Martin knew that philosophy held the key to his puzzle. He struggled to put these ideas together to form his own philosophy.

Some of the philosophers Martin studied believed in pacifism. A pacifist is someone who does not believe that using violence is the way to solve problems. Pacifists refuse to fight even when someone is violent toward them. While Martin agreed with this idea, he wondered how it would work in certain situations. He thought about how the Nazis, led by Germany's leader Adolf Hitler, had just murdered millions of Jews. Many countries had joined together during World War II to defeat Hitler. Martin wondered how a pacifist could refuse to fight an action as evil as the one the Nazis had just committed. But through his reading, Martin realized that being a pacifist didn't mean simply doing nothing to stop evil. Instead, he now understood, it meant fighting evil in a nonviolent way.

Martin began to understand what Gandhi had said about fighting evil with love. He thought about the white student who had hated him because he was black. They had become friends because Martin refused to hate him back. Martin decided that fighting hatred with hatred only makes the hate stronger. That was why Jesus had said, "Love your enemies" and "Turn the other cheek."

Martin finally put enough pieces of the puzzle together to come up with his own philosophy. He decided that evil wasn't just some force that existed in a society and made people bad. He believed that people could control evil by finding the evil within themselves. They could get rid of evil in society only if they first got rid of it within themselves. With this philosophy, along with pacifism, Martin had found a way to fight evil in the world.

CORETTA AND THE RETURN TO THE SOUTH

"We are [all] tied in a single garment of destiny. Whatever affects one directly, affects all indirectly. As long as there is poverty in the world, no man can be totally rich. . . . I can never be what I ought to be until you are what you ought to be. You can never be what you ought to be until I am what I ought to be."

MARTIN LUTHER KING, JR.

During his first year at Boston University, King began looking for a wife. A friend from Atlanta told him about Coretta Scott. Coretta was pretty and intelligent, but, the friend warned, she didn't go to church very often.

Martin called Coretta. She wasn't thrilled to have a Baptist minister calling her. She wasn't interested in any stuffed shirt who was going to try to tell her how to behave. But Martin convinced her to have lunch with him. When they met, Coretta thought he was short and dull. Martin liked Coretta's smile, her hair, and her quiet confidence. They told each other a bit about themselves. They discovered that they were both from the South.

Coretta was born on a farm outside of Marion, Alabama, about 80 miles from Montgomery, the state capital. Her father, Obadiah, and her mother, Bernice, had built up a successful chicken farm of several hundred acres. They now owned a small trucking company, a filling station, and a grocery store as well. As a child, however, Coretta had picked cotton in her family's fields and washed their clothes in a washtub. She went to a "colored" school with outdoor toilets until the family could afford to send her to a private church school nearby.

After attending Antioch College in Ohio, Coretta received a small scholarship to the New England Conservatory of Music in Boston. She intended to have a career as a classical singer. In exchange for room and board, she worked as a maid at the boardinghouse where she lived.

Coretta and Martin discovered that they both loved music, books, and talking about ideas. Most important, they both believed in fighting injustice toward African Americans.

After they had dated for a few months, Martin asked Coretta to marry him. Coretta hesitated, but not because she didn't love Martin. The problem was that she would have to make a choice between a career as a singer and a career as his wife. Like other men during the 1950s, King felt that a husband and a wife had certain duties in the family. He thought the husband should bring in the money and the wife should stay at home and take care of the house and the family.

To Coretta, becoming a homemaker and a preacher's wife seemed a full-time, boring job. She wrote to her sister Edythe for advice. Edythe had met Martin, and she wrote to Coretta,

telling her to go ahead and marry Martin if she loved him. Coretta might not have the career she dreamed of, her sister wrote, but she would certainly have a career. "You will not be marrying any ordinary young minister," Edythe predicted.

Martin gave Coretta certain tests in order to find out how well she did some things, such as cooking. He questioned her about how she would treat different kinds of people who might someday make up his congregation. Coretta passed all of Martin's "tests." The last one was meeting Martin's family.

The visit with Martin's parents was worse than Coretta had expected. Mrs. King was polite but very cold. At first Daddy King paid no attention to Coretta. Then he told her that his son was already promised to a number of women. What's more, he would be the one to decide who M.L. married, and it would be someone who was better for his son than he thought Coretta was.

M.L.'s wife would be someone who had "much to share and much to offer," he said.

At this point Coretta became angry. "I have something to offer, too," she stated.

Martin just sat there, saying nothing. Coretta couldn't believe it. She didn't know that he had told his mother he was planning to marry her. He knew that Mrs. King would pass this information along to Daddy King. Martin also knew that Daddy King would need time to accept his choice, and this was one confrontation he wanted to avoid. Fortunately, Daddy King was secretly impressed with Coretta's strength. By the time the visit was over, he acted as if their marriage was all his idea. On June 18, 1953, Daddy King married Martin and Coretta on the lawn of the Scotts' home.

Back in Boston, the couple rented a four-room apartment and got back to studying. Coretta had to take 13 courses that year in order to graduate in 1954. Since she was so busy, Martin cleaned the apartment and washed their clothes, hanging them in the kitchen to dry. He cooked their evening meal every Thursday. His specialty was pork chops, cabbage, and pigs' feet.

That summer, King worked on his Ph.D. thesis, a long paper that he had to write in order to get his doctoral degree. He also looked for a job. Offers came from several universities, including Morehouse College. Three churches also contacted him. The offer that most interested him came from the Dexter Avenue Baptist Church in Montgomery, Alabama. After a Christmas visit with his family, King drove to the church to preach a trial sermon.

The Dexter Avenue Baptist Church had only about 300 members, but they were wealthy and important citizens. The church was known for its educated ministers. Dexter's congregation was very impressed with King's sermon. They couldn't get over the fact that such a young man could deliver such a smart sermon. In March 1954, Dexter's board of directors sent a telegram to King saying they had chosen him to be their pastor. They offered him the highest salary received by any black minister in Montgomery at that time.

Martin and Coretta now had a serious decision to make. They had both fled the South, where they were considered "second-class citizens." Jim Crow still ruled there, with one set of rules for whites and another set for blacks. What about raising their children there? they wondered. Martin remembered the pain he had felt when his best friend couldn't play with him anymore because he was "colored." He remembered entering Morehouse College and the shock of learning that he could read only at the level of an eighth grader. Their children would be forced to attend all-black schools and receive the same inferior education he had received. And what about Coretta's musical career? There were far better opportunities for her in the North.

After many days and nights of discussion, the Kings decided to return to the South. Perhaps they could find some solution to the terrible conditions that existed for African Americans there. Besides, they had the feeling that "something remarkable was unfolding in the South, and we wanted to be on hand to witness it."

Something remarkable *was* happening in the South. It would affect not only the South but the entire United States. In May 1954, Thurgood Marshall, a black lawyer, and the NAACP Legal Defense Fund won a landmark victory in the courts. The Supreme Court ruled on the NAACP case *Brown* v. *Board of Education of Topeka, Kansas*. This ruling outlawed segregation in public schools. It stated that having separate schools for black children and white children was illegal.

The 1954 *Brown* v. *Board of Education* ruling overturned the 1896 *Plessy* v. *Ferguson* case that had made "separate but equal" legal. If segregation in schools was now unconstitutional, segregation in other places would also become unconstitutional. It was just a matter of time before the Court ruled on them, too. This decision outraged segregationists, especially those in the South. They called the day on which the ruling was handed down Black Monday.

During that same month, Martin Luther King, Jr., preached his first sermon as the pastor of the Dexter Avenue Baptist Church. He and Coretta visited the black section where "we would be living without choice." They saw blacks crowded into the back of buses. Coretta would have to ride these buses when Martin was using their car. Had they made the right decision? they wondered.

Needless to say, Daddy King wasn't thrilled with Martin and Coretta's decision. Why were they going to such a small church? he demanded to know. Why were they going to a city where trouble between blacks and whites was worse than it was in Atlanta? Why? Martin was already in line for the position of pastor of the Ebenezer Baptist Church where his father was pastor. It was as if Martin had rejected Daddy King, and in a way he had. Daddy King wouldn't allow Martin to be a grown-up. Martin still needed to shape his own life, and he felt he had to do this away from his overbearing father.

The Kings settled into their new life in Montgomery. Each morning Martin rose at five-thirty and spent three hours working on his thesis. Then he showered and shaved, and had breakfast with Coretta at nine o'clock. He spent the rest of the day taking care of his church duties. Coretta sang in the choir, attended meetings, and visited church members.

Each week King spent a full 15 hours writing his sermons. At first he preached to his people as if they were a classroom of students. Then he began to understand that they needed more than just lessons about heaven and earth. They needed to express their feelings about God and the world. They also needed him to help them do this.

The church had long been one of the only places that belonged to African Americans. For some reason, a black church wasn't threatening to whites, so it became a place of safety for blacks. The church became the place where African Americans gathered socially and made important community decisions. In church they didn't have to behave in a certain way. They could express their sorrows and their joys. They could find relief from hatred and bitterness, and strength to face the next day in a segregated society.

King realized that part of his job was to help his congregation "let go." In order to do that he, too, would have to let go. He began adding some "whooping" to his sermons, and the people responded to him with an "Amen!" or "Tell it!" or "That's right!" Each time he called out and the congregation answered him, the emotion in the church grew. King realized that each time his people responded to him, he became more excited.

It dawned on him that this was his father's style of preaching. Once King had been embarrassed by this form of preaching. Once he had thought it wasn't very helpful. Now he saw just how helpful it was—not only to the congregation but to himself as well.

As the Kings became more involved in the community, they learned more about how blacks and whites in Montgomery lived. Like the rest of the South, they lived in separate sections of the city. They used two different taxi services and rode at separate ends of the same bus. If blacks were allowed to shop in the same stores as whites, they often had to wait until all the whites had been served.

Most blacks in Montgomery worked in white homes and businesses. This included nearly two-thirds of the women and half of the men. They toiled as cooks, gardeners, maids, drivers, elevator operators, and dishwashers.

When the Kings went to Montgomery in 1954, there were 30,000 blacks in the county who were of voting age. But only 2,000 of them were registered. At the registration office, there were separate lines for blacks and whites. Blacks had to fill out long forms. They were required to pass difficult tests in order to prove that they could read and write. These tests were not given to whites.

King was shocked to see how easily blacks accepted this unjust treatment. What made him saddest, however, was "a lack of self-respect. Many unconsciously wondered whether they actually deserved any better conditions," he said.

There were 50 black churches in Montgomery, but as far as King could tell, most of the ministers weren't doing much to change the conditions under which African Americans in the city lived. Ministers had long been the leaders of the black community—not only spiritually but also politically. However, they were still more concerned about getting people to heaven than about helping them here on earth. Martin met one minister, though, who felt much the same as he did—Rev. Ralph Abernathy.

In many ways, Abernathy and King were very different. Abernathy was one of 12 children born to a poor sharecropper in Alabama. He had attended all-black schools in the South, graduating from Alabama State College and Atlanta University. He wasn't as sophisticated as his friend King, nor was he a brilliant speaker. But Abernathy was just as determined as King to bring about change for African Americans.

King admired Abernathy because he had worked his way up from poverty and become a strong leader. King had been born with certain advantages and had never had to struggle as Abernathy had. To King, "Ab" had earned his right to leadership. The two preachers soon became fast friends.

In the spring of 1955, King finished his thesis and received his doctoral degree from Boston University. He was now Dr. King. Soon, Coretta told him, he would be adding another title to his name—that of father. That year there were many events that touched the Kings and the rest of the country as well. The Supreme Court handed down its second ruling on the *Brown* v. *Board of Education* case. This ruling stated how segregation should be ended in all public schools in the United States. This 1955 Court ruling left it up to each state to desegregate its schools "with all deliberate speed." What that actually meant was that a state could take as long as it wanted to integrate its schools. The Supreme Court had backed down!

Ralph Abernathy (left) and his friend Martin Luther King, Jr., in Montgomery

During the summer of 1955, news of a brutal murder filled the newspapers. A 14-year-old black boy named Emmett Till was killed while visiting relatives in Money, Mississippi. Emmett was from Chicago. The way blacks and whites behaved toward each other in Chicago was very different from the way they behaved in the South. As Emmett and his friends were leaving a grocery store, he called out to a white woman, "Bye, baby." It was only a joke.

According to later accounts, the woman's husband and another white man dragged Emmett away from his uncle's house. They beat him to make him apologize. When he wouldn't, they tied a 70-pound fan to his neck with barbed wire and made him carry it to the bank of the Tallahatchie River. There one of them shot him in the head and threw his body into the river.

When Emmett was found, his mother put his mutilated body on display at a funeral home in Chicago. She wanted the world to see what white hatred in the South had done to her son. The nation was shocked at the photos they saw. All the same, an all-white jury found Emmett Till's killers not guilty. One white man couldn't understand why everyone was so upset about one dead black person. "That river's full of niggers," he said.

This was the South where Martin and Coretta King were afraid to bring up their children. Nevertheless, here they were. In November, their first child was born. It was a girl—Yolanda. They called her Yoki. Only a few weeks after Yoki was born, King received a phone call that would change his life as well as the lives of his family forever.

WALKING FOR FREEDOM

"There comes a time when people get tired of being trampled by oppression.... The story of [the bus boycott in] Montgomery is the story of 50,000 such Negroes who were willing to substitute tired feet for tired souls."

MARTIN LUTHER KING, JR.

"My feets is tired, but my soul is rested."

SISTER POLLARD, citizen of Montgomery

Without even saying hello, a gruff voice began talking as soon as King picked up the phone on Friday, December 2, 1955. It was E. D. Nixon, a local NAACP leader. Nixon told King that his former NAACP secretary, Rosa Parks, had been arrested the night before, on December 1. She had refused to give a white man her seat on the public bus.

Rosa Parks had been returning home after a long day at the Montgomery department store where she worked as a tailor's assistant. She was tired and glad to find an empty seat. However, at the next stop several whites got on and one man was left standing. The bus driver called back to the blacks sitting in the middle section. "Y'd better make it light on yourselves and let me have those seats," he shouted. Three blacks rose. When Parks refused, she was arrested for breaking the law that banned integrated seating on the city's buses.

E. D. Nixon visited Parks that night after she was released on bail. He told her that the NAACP wanted to test the bus segregation law. They hoped that if she was found guilty she would allow the NAACP to appeal her case, or take it to a higher court. If the NAACP could get the case to a higher court, they might be able to overturn the segregation laws. Rosa Parks's mother and husband were afraid that she would be killed for doing this sort of thing. But Mrs. Parks, an active member of the NAACP, was tired of not standing up for her rights. She agreed.

Nixon told King about another plan he had for fighting segregation on the buses—a boycott. If African Americans boycotted, or stopped riding, the buses, the bus company would lose a lot of money. Then the company would have to listen to their demands.

Nixon and the Women's Political Council had been trying to organize a boycott for some time. On the night Rosa Parks was arrested, he contacted Jo Ann Robinson, a member of the council. Robinson printed 35,000 leaflets that very night to distribute all over the city that weekend. The leaflets asked the blacks of Montgomery not to ride the buses on Monday, December 5, to protest segregation and Rosa Parks's arrest.

Nixon had convinced about 20 black ministers to meet that evening at the Dexter Avenue Baptist Church to discuss a boy-

Rosa Parks on her way into court in Montgomery, Alabama, during the bus boycott.

cott. King was happily surprised when about 45 showed up. The ministers agreed to announce the boycott in their churches the Sunday before it was scheduled to begin. Then they would all meet again on Monday night to decide whether to continue it.

On the night before the boycott, King's phone rang and rang with last-minute plans. Eight African-American taxi companies had agreed to provide 60 to 70 taxis to transport boycotters for only 10 cents—the same as the bus fare. But King was nervous about whether the community would pull together. If the boycott fizzled out, the whites would make fun of blacks and treat them even worse. At midnight the phones stopped ringing, and the Kings fell asleep "with a strange mixture of hope and anxiety."

"Martin, Martin, come quickly!" Coretta called out. It was six o'clock on Monday morning, and King was in the kitchen having coffee. He rushed to their living room. From the front window they could see an empty bus passing. Fifteen minutes later, a second bus rolled by. This bus was also empty.

King jumped into his car and drove down the main streets. He saw only eight black riders during the morning rush hour. "A miracle had taken place!" he wrote later.

The afternoon rush hour was the same. The sidewalks were jammed with African Americans walking. Many of them were elderly people who had to travel as much as 12 miles to and from work. Some people thumbed rides; a few even rode on mules and in horse-drawn buggies. People gathered at the bus stops, cheering the empty buses as they pulled away.

That morning Rosa Parks was found guilty of disobeying the segregation law and fined $14. Her lawyers were delighted. If she had been found not guilty, everything would be over. They immediately appealed her case to a higher court where they could test the law.

Around three o'clock on Monday afternoon, several black leaders met to plan the mass meeting for that evening. The boycott would probably continue, and they needed to organize and choose leaders. King was surprised to hear his name mentioned as a possible head of the new organization, which would be called the Montgomery Improvement Association (MIA). Things were happening so quickly that he found himself agreeing before he had time to think.

King drove home and told his wife what had happened. His first duty as president of the MIA was to give a speech at the meeting that night. It would have to be the best and clearest speech he had ever given. The people needed direction. Reporters would be there. Whatever he said might be heard all across the nation. He would have to set a good example for his people.

King was beginning to panic. It usually took him 15 hours to write a sermon. Now he was being asked to prepare an important speech in only 20 minutes. He jotted down some notes. Then it was time to leave for the Holt Street Baptist Church, where the meeting was being held.

The traffic around the church was so heavy that King had to park his car four blocks away. The church had already been filled, and now 4,000 people were overflowing onto the streets outside. Loudspeakers had been set up so they could hear what was being said inside.

When King was called to the podium, he talked about the insults and abuses that African Americans had suffered on the buses. "But there comes a time that people get tired," he said. "We are here this evening to say to those who have mistreated us so long that we are tired—tired of being segregated and humiliated, tired of being kicked about by the brutal feet of oppression....

"If we are wrong," he continued, "the Supreme Court of this nation is wrong. If we are wrong, the Constitution of the United States is wrong. If we are wrong, God Almighty is wrong.... If we are wrong, justice is a lie."

He urged the people to act peacefully. He asked them not to force anyone to stay off the buses. He told them to respond to violence only with the Christian rule of "Love thy enemy." "If we fail to do this," he told them, "our protest will end up as a meaningless drama on the stage of history.... In spite of the mistreatment that we have confronted, we must not become bitter and end up by hating our white brothers. As Booker T. Washington said, 'Let no man pull you so low as to make you hate him.' "

King's rich baritone voice rolled out: "If you will protest courageously, and yet with dignity and Christian love, when the history books are written in future generations, the historian will have to pause and say, 'There lived a great people—a black people—who injected new meaning and dignity into the veins of civilization.' This is our challenge and our overwhelming responsibility."

King went to his chair trembling. Somehow all of his beliefs had come together here tonight in this 16-minute speech. As he sat down, the people rose to their feet, clapping, yelling, and waving their arms. He was amazed. This speech had gotten more response than had all of his carefully prepared sermons.

Then Rosa Parks, the symbol of the people's hope and courage, was introduced. After that Ralph Abernathy read the MIA's demands. They wanted seating on buses to be open to everyone—black and white. They wanted bus drivers to treat black passengers with respect. And they wanted the bus company to hire some black drivers on the bus lines that serviced largely black areas. "All in favor of the motion, stand," Abernathy concluded. Every single person there rose immediately, shouting for joy.

Watching them, King thought they had already won, no matter how long it took them to get their demands met. "The real victory was in the mass meeting, where thousands of black people stood revealed with a new sense of dignity and destiny," he later wrote.

At their first meeting with the MIA, the city officials said that it would be impossible to meet the MIA's demands without breaking segregation laws. Now the boycott was really on. The MIA's first job was to find another way for the people to get to and from work.

They could no longer use taxis. The city had informed them that there was a law against charging less than 45 cents a ride. This would make taxis too expensive. King called Rev. Theodore Jemison, who had led a bus boycott earlier in Baton Rouge, Louisiana. Jemison told him how to set up a private car pool.

Within a few days, more than 300 people had volunteered their time or their cars. At first cars just drove around town picking up anyone. By December 13, however, the MIA had worked out a system complete with pickup and drop-off stations. Even the city officials had to admit that this new transportation system was better than theirs.

Some people preferred to walk, however. They knew that just the sight of them walking every day gave a signal to the world that the times were changing. There were certain conditions that African Americans simply wouldn't accept anymore. One driver noticed an elderly woman hobbling along and pulled up beside her. "Jump in, grandmother," he called. "You don't need to walk." But she just waved him on. "I'm not walking for myself," she replied. "I'm walking for my children and my grandchildren."

Because of the TV coverage, people all over the world learned about the courage of the Montgomery boycotters. Letters and money came from everywhere—even from the crew of a ship in the middle of the ocean. Finally, the MIA had to hire a staff of 10 and set up an office to handle everything. The MIA also held mass meetings twice a week. As they planned their next moves, people gathered strength from one another at these meetings.

By December 19, the MIA had met with city officials and the bus company three times. It was clear that the city officials weren't taking the boycott seriously. Wait until the first day it rains, they said, laughing. Then we'll see who gets back on the buses. Well, it rained—and it snowed—and the people still walked.

When city officials began to realize that the boycott wasn't a joke, they began to spread lies about King. They said he was putting MIA money into his own pockets and had bought two new cars. They tried to make older blacks angry by saying that young ministers like King were taking their place as leaders of the protest.

Some MIA leaders were already jealous of all the publicity King was getting. When they began complaining that King was using the movement for his own glory, King was so hurt that he offered to resign. But no one really wanted him to leave. He was doing a good job, and the people wouldn't follow anyone else. He had an almost magical effect on them. King had a gift "for giving people the feeling that they could be bigger and stronger

Martin Luther King, Jr., with his wife, Coretta, after his release from jail during the boycott.

and more courageous and more loving than they thought they could be," said one MIA member.

When their trick to get rid of King didn't work, city officials began harassing him. One January evening he was arrested and taken to jail for going just a few miles over the speed limit. This was the first time King had ever been in jail. He felt powerless and terrified. While "Ab" tried to post bail for him, a group of angry blacks gathered outside. Alarmed, the police quickly released King.

The harassment didn't stop, however. King received 30 to 40 hate letters every day. They contained such messages as, "You niggers are getting [yourselves] in a bad place.... we need... a Hitler to get our country straightened out." The phone calls—as many as 30 a day—were worse. Sometimes the only sound would be that of someone spitting into a receiver. Coretta couldn't take the phone off the hook for fear of missing an important call. Every time the phone rang, she jumped.

King began to fear for his life and for his family's safety. He realized that there were people who wanted him out of the way and that it would be very easy for them to kill him and his family. Late one night the phone rang and King picked it up before it could wake Coretta. "Listen, nigger," an ugly voice snarled, "we've taken all we want from you; before next week you'll be sorry you ever came to Montgomery." Click.

King hung up and tried to go back to sleep, but "all of my fears had come down on me at once," he said. He went into the kitchen to figure out how he could quit as the leader of the MIA. He had never felt so afraid or alone, not even when Mama died.

He bowed his head over the kitchen table and began to pray out loud: "I am here taking a stand for what I believe is right. But now I am afraid. The people are looking to me for leadership, and if I stand before them without strength and courage, they too will falter. I am at the end of my powers. I have nothing left. I've come to the point where I can't face it alone."

Suddenly it seemed to King that God was speaking to him through an inner voice. The voice said, "Stand up for righteousness, stand up for truth; and God will be at your side forever." A calm came over King. Even though he had been a minister for several years, this was the first time he had ever felt that God was truly a part of him. His fears began to melt away. He was ready to face anything now.

Three days later, King had to face one of his worst fears. His house was bombed. He raced home to find that the entire front of the house had been blown away. Fortunately, Coretta and Yoki had been in the back. Hundreds of angry blacks gathered outside the house. All the white reporters, politicians, and even the police officers on the scene were afraid for their lives.

King walked out onto the porch and held up his hand. Complete silence fell. He told the crowd that he and his family were all right and that they should all leave peacefully. "If you have weapons, take them home; if you do not have them, please do not seek to get them. . . . We must meet violence with nonviolence. . . . We must love our white brothers no matter what they do to us. . . . We must meet hate with love. Remember, if I am stopped, this movement will not stop, because God is with the movement."

The crowd was stunned. This man's house had just been bombed; his family could have been killed. Yet he was standing on the ruins of his front porch telling them to love those who had done the terrible deed. Suddenly there were shouts of "Amen!" and "We are with you all the way, Reverend." Then the crowd began to break up quietly.

But it took King a while to believe his own words. That night he lay awake trying to understand the whites who had done this awful thing. He realized that they had probably been taught to believe that what they had done was right. Their parents, schools, communities, books, even their churches, had taught them so. They were trying to hold on to the only way of living they knew. Finally he was able to forgive them.

All this violence was too much for Daddy King, however. He insisted that Martin and Coretta move to Atlanta.

"My friends and associates are being arrested," King told his father. "I would rather be in jail ten years than desert my people now. I have begun the struggle, and I can't turn back." There was an awful silence for a moment; then Daddy King broke down and sobbed. King couldn't bear to hurt his father like this, but he had reached the point of no return.

A couple of weeks later, King and 88 other boycott leaders were arrested for breaking an old antiboycott law. The boycott was interfering with a lawful business without "just cause," they were told. The leaders were jubilant when they were all found guilty. Now they could take their case to a federal court and test the antiboycott law.

In the federal court, the MIA lawyers asked the court to end all bus segregation because it was unconstitutional. In June, the federal court ruled in the MIA's favor. The Montgomery city lawyers then appealed the case to the Supreme Court, the highest court in the land. This was exactly what the MIA wanted.

City officials harassed the boycotters as they waited at pick-up stations. They threatened to arrest car-pool drivers and cancel their car insurance. Finally, in October they tried to have the car pool declared illegal. They claimed that it was hurting the bus company. The city demanded $15,000 in damages from the MIA for the boycott. Things looked bad. Without the car pool, the people would lose their only form of transportation. Was it fair to ask the people to walk in cold, snowy weather? King wondered. Even worse, what if they lost the boycott and the whole year of proud protest proved to be all in vain?

November 13, 1956, was the day of the car-pool trial. King was sure that the white judge would rule in the city's favor—they always did. During lunch a reporter ran up to King waving a newspaper. "Here is the decision that you have been waiting for!" he said. King couldn't believe his eyes. The newspaper said the Supreme Court had declared that Alabama's laws requiring segregation on buses were unconstitutional. The boycotters had won.

When they returned to the courtroom, the scene was a joke to King. The judge ruled that the car pool had to be stopped, just as King knew he would. But it didn't matter. The Supreme Court ruling had already made the car pool unnecessary.

The next night there was a huge celebration at the Holt Street Baptist Church, where the boycott had begun. The audience wept, shouted, and clapped for joy. When King mounted the platform to speak, he waited for the room to become quiet.

"I would be terribly disappointed if any of you go back to the buses bragging, 'We, the Negroes, won a victory over the white people,' " he said sternly. "We must not take this as a victory over the white man but as a victory for justice and democracy. We must not go back on the buses and push people around. . . . We must simply sit where there is a vacant seat." The MIA issued rules and guidelines to help people integrate the buses peacefully. The city did nothing, hoping that violence would occur. This would make the boycotters look bad.

On December 20, the Supreme Court ruling finally became legal in Montgomery. The next day King, Abernathy, Nixon, and Glen Smiley, a white minister, sat together in the first integrated bus. In spite of some violent reaction by whites, the city gradually desegregated its bus system.

Martin Luther King, Jr., helped the African-American people of Montgomery win more than the right to sit anywhere they wanted to sit on a bus. Before the boycott, many of them were afraid. But they had fought for their rights and won, and they had done so without raising a hand or striking a single blow. As an African-American janitor told a reporter, "We got our heads up now, and we won't ever bow down again—no sir—except before God!"

THE PREACHER LEADS A MOVEMENT

"It is not enough for the church to be active in the realm of ideas; it must move out into the arena of social action. First, the church must remove the yoke of segregation from its own body. ... The most segregated hour of Christian America is eleven o'clock on Sunday morning. ... The most segregated school ... is the Sunday School."

MARTIN LUTHER KING, JR.

The Montgomery bus boycott had made Martin Luther King, Jr., a household name by 1957. The 27-year-old preacher from Montgomery was on the cover of *Time* magazine. Other important and popular magazines ran interviews on him. In these interviews, King outlined what he thought were the next steps his people had to take in their struggle for equality. First, they had to secure the right to vote. Second, they must work for legislation that would guarantee their rights and protect them from racial hatred. Third, they should invest their money in themselves by starting their own businesses or buying from African-American businesses.

King was suddenly considered the most learned African-American leader in the United States, and he was worried about his quick rise to fame. "People will expect me to perform miracles for the rest of my life," he told Coretta. But his rise to fame had only just begun.

While the Montgomery boycott was taking place, other bus boycotts had sprung up in Florida and Alabama. It looked as if a movement had begun in the South. King met with 60 African-American leaders from 10 southern states to form an organization that would unite this movement.

Other groups were fighting racism in other parts of the country. The National Urban League, founded in 1911, concentrated on improving conditions for African Americans in the northern cities. The Congress of Racial Equality (CORE) had been working in the northern cities since 1942. The NAACP's battles in the courts were also helping African Americans more in the North. But African Americans in the South felt that they needed a new organization to deal with their special problems.

Since southern black ministers were the most powerful leaders of their people, it was agreed that the members of this new organization should come from the church. Its goal would be to expand "the Montgomery Way" throughout the South. At a conference held on January 10 and 11, 1957, the Southern Christian Leadership Conference (SCLC) was formed. There was no question who the president of the organization would be—Martin Luther King, Jr.

Running the SCLC's main office in Atlanta, Georgia, was Ella Baker. Baker was a strong-willed woman who had worked for the NAACP for 20 years. One of her jobs at the NAACP was going from town to town throughout the South to convince African Americans to join the organization. This was a very dangerous job.

Baker had her own ideas about how the SCLC should be run. Sometimes these ideas clashed with those of the male leaders. For example, she thought it would be fairer if the organization was run by everyone who belonged to it rather than by just one leader. She thought the SCLC and the press gave King too much attention and power.

King was indeed the most famous member of the SCLC. People all over the world knew who he was, including Kwame Nkrumah, the new prime minister of Ghana in West Africa. Ghana had just won its independence from Britain, and Nkrumah invited Martin and Coretta King to attend the celebrations in March.

On their way home, the Kings went through Nigeria, a nation in West Africa that was also controlled by Britain. They were shocked at the poverty and suffering they saw there. Conditions there were worse than those in the most backward rural parts of the South. King was heartsick. Even though he had been raised with plenty, he always identified with the poor.

He was also furious. To him the British were taking advantage of Africans in much the same way American colonists and slave owners had used black slaves. At that time, a dozen African countries were beginning to win their independence from European countries. King felt that the attempts of blacks in Africa to throw off white rule was similar to the civil rights movement blacks in the United States had started.

A few months after King returned from West Africa, the first civil rights bill since 1875 was passed. It established the Civil Rights Commission to advise the president on civil rights issues. This Civil Rights Act of 1957 also gave the federal government the right to sue registration offices in the South if they discriminated against blacks over voting rights. But King didn't think the bill went far enough. It didn't give the government the power to enforce school desegregation and other rights that had already been established.

In the meantime, Central High School in Little Rock, Arkansas, had become the center of a battle over one of the rights that had already been won—the right to attend a desegregated school. After the Supreme Court ruling that segregated schools were unconstitutional, a federal court ordered Central High School to integrate. Nine students—called the Little Rock Nine—were to enter Central that September. Arkansas's Governor Orval Faubus placed National Guardsmen around the school—not to protect the children but to keep them out. For safety, the children were all to travel to school together that first day. However, one of them, 15-year-old Elizabeth Eckford, wasn't aware of the arrangement.

As Elizabeth walked toward the school, she was met by a crowd of furious whites. Their faces twisted in hate, they cursed and threatened her. When she tried to pass through the line of guards, they wouldn't move to let her by. Suddenly somebody started yelling, "Lynch her! Lynch her!" Everywhere Elizabeth turned to get away, the mob chased her, snarling, "No nigger bitch is going to get in our school." Finally a friendly white woman managed to guide her away. When a bus rolled by, they quickly jumped on it.

Each time the nine students tried to enter the school, whites threatened to attack them as well as the police. Finally, President Dwight D. Eisenhower sent in more than 1,000 army soldiers to escort the black students to Central. The Little Rock Nine had to be taken to school surrounded by jeeps mounted with machine guns.

The incident showed the people across the United States that winning racial freedom in the courts was one thing, but winning it in the schools, the workplace, and public places would be another matter.

In October 1957, the Kings' second child, Martin Luther King III, was born. King was so busy that he hardly had any

The Little Rock Nine, under the protection of federal troops, desegregated Central High School.

time to spend with little Marty. During the next year, he worked on a book about the Montgomery bus boycott, called *Stride Toward Freedom*. On top of that, he traveled all over the country making speeches to raise money for the SCLC, the NAACP, CORE, and other black organizations. One speech delivered by him seemed to get more results than 25 speeches made by other leaders. King made people believe that they could change their lives. He used all the big words he had learned and talked about all the philosophies he had studied. But when he spoke, even those who had never been to school could understand what he was saying.

In September 1958, King's book *Stride Toward Freedom* was published. The reviews were good, and he was now in even greater demand to appear on radio and TV. Unfortunately, his fame made him an easy target for all kinds of emotions. One afternoon as he sat in a store signing copies of his book, a woman stabbed him in the chest with a letter opener.

Surgeons had to take out one of King's ribs and part of his breastbone in order to remove the letter opener. If he had sneezed before the surgery, the letter opener would have gone through the main artery from his heart and killed him. King later found out that his attacker was mentally ill. Instead of calling for her punishment, he told the police to "get her healed."

While King was in the hospital, thousands of letters poured in from people of all races. One ninth grader wrote: "While it should not matter, I would like to mention that I am a white girl. . . . I'm so happy that you didn't sneeze."

That winter King had recovered enough to make a trip to India with Coretta. He wanted to better understand Gandhi. He wanted to see the country in which his hero had brought about a nonviolent revolution. What he saw—poverty, filth, hunger—shocked him more than Nigeria had. He saw millions of people in rags carrying their belongings in newspapers and eating whatever they could find in garbage piles. At night they wrapped themselves in filthy blankets and slept in the streets.

Everywhere the Kings went, there were beggars. King was told not to give them money, but he couldn't bear not to. "What can you do when an old haggard woman or a little crippled urchin comes up and motions to you that she is hungry?" Why couldn't these people have the surplus grain the United States had stored away? he demanded in later speeches.

In New Delhi, India's capital, King placed a wreath on the shrine where Gandhi had been cremated. Later he met with Prime Minister Jawaharlal Nehru, who told him about India's caste system. A caste is a rank that is given to people in India. People who belonged to low castes were called untouchables because many members of the high castes believed they would be dirtied if they even touched such a person.

India's new constitution prohibited discrimination against untouchables. The government spent millions of dollars trying to improve the living conditions of the untouchables. In addition, if two people belonging to a high caste and a low caste were competing for the same job or place in college, the law said the person of low caste had to get the position.

Nehru was asked whether he didn't think this treatment of high castes was also prejudiced. Nehru said that it may have been, but it was a way to make up for the years of injustices that had been done to the people of low castes. Why couldn't the United States do this? King wondered. Both countries had passed laws against discrimination. But while India was acting upon its laws, the United States government had to be forced to treat blacks fairly.

Back at home, King looked at the situation in the South. It was grim. He was most concerned about the lack of voting rights. Throughout the South, there were 5 million eligible African-American voters, but only 1.3 million were registered. King wanted the barriers that kept these voters from registering removed. He believed that those millions of votes could change the way politicians responded to the people's needs. Under him, the SCLC decided to file complaints about voter registration with the newly formed Civil Rights Commission.

King also wanted the SCLC to start programs that would teach people how to protest in nonviolent ways. He hoped these people would then spread out into other communities and teach others. In this way, people all over the South would be involved in this nonviolent movement. To do this, King planned to enlarge the staff of the SCLC.

This was a big step for the SCLC. It was also a turning point for King. After discussing everything with Coretta, he had decided to become a full-time leader in this new civil rights movement. In order to do that, he and Coretta would have to move to Atlanta, Georgia, where the SCLC's headquarters was located. He could earn a living there as a pastor at the Ebenezer Baptist Church. Unfortunately, this meant that he would have to leave the Dexter Avenue Baptist Church. It was a painful decision. But King's congregation was now larger than any single church. He had found a new way to put his message of Christian love into action all over the South and perhaps throughout the entire country.

On Sunday, November 29, 1959, King told his congregation that he would be leaving Montgomery. He and the congregation wept as he told them: "I have come to the conclusion that I can't stop now. History has thrust upon me a responsibility from which I cannot turn away."

IN THE VALLEY OF THE SHADOW OF DEATH

"Even though morality cannot be legislated, behavior can be regulated.... It may be true that the law can't make a man love me, but it can keep him from lynching me."

MARTIN LUTHER KING, JR.

The Kings moved back to Atlanta, Georgia, in January 1960 in order to work in the movement full-time. A month later, King watched proudly as college students began their own movement. On February 1, 1960, four college students sat down at the lunch counter in a Woolworth's store in Greensboro, North Carolina. For blacks, sitting at the counter was against the law. They could buy food at the lunch counter, but they had to stand up to eat. They weren't allowed to sit next to white customers.

These Greensboro students were aware of this law, and they didn't expect to be served. They simply sat there quietly to call attention to this form of prejudice. During the next few days, more students came. It wasn't easy to just sit. White shoppers screamed curses in the students' faces and shoved them. But the students remained nonviolent and continued their quiet protest.

News of the sit-ins spread to other colleges. In 1942, CORE had staged sit-ins, but this was the first time this kind of protest had made the headlines. Within two months, there had been 50 sit-ins across the South. Sometimes businesses would close down rather than serve blacks. White customers poured sugar, ketchup, and hot coffee on the protesters, and burned them with cigarettes. On top of that, protesters were often put in jail.

King admired the students' nonviolent protests. He answered hundreds of letters from colleges all over the South, giving students advice. He always encouraged them to protest "the Montgomery Way."

Ella Baker was also proud of the students. They were creating the kind of movement she wanted—one that sprang up wherever action was needed, one that didn't have a single leader telling everyone what to do. Both Baker and King felt that the students needed to organize, however. Baker convinced King to donate SCLC funds for a student conference at Shaw University in Raleigh, North Carolina. On April 15, 1960, more than 200 students gathered there—from the North as well as the South.

Both the SCLC and the NAACP wanted the students to join their organizations. But Baker urged the young people to develop their own group so that they would be free of adults telling them how to run things. In the end, the students agreed with their "spiritual mother." They formed the Student Nonviolent Coordinating Committee, (SNCC, pronounced "snick"). King served on SNCC's Adult Advisory Committee, helped raise money for them, and provided office space for the group in SCLC headquarters.

Whites pour ketchup and sugar on sit-in demonstrators in Jackson, Mississippi.

In Atlanta, King sat-in with the students and was arrested along with them. After a few days the students were released, but King was held for violating probation on a minor traffic ticket he had received months earlier. He was given an outrageous sentence of four months' hard labor in one of Georgia's work camps. Many blacks who went there had never returned.

That night King was awakened. The guards handcuffed his wrists, put chains around his ankles, and threw him into the back of a car. They drove for hours to Reidsville State Prison, about 250 miles from Atlanta. King was terrified. The guards there were known to be vicious, and he was miles away from anyone who could help him.

Not long after King arrived, he was mysteriously released and flown back to Atlanta. There King learned that Senator Jonn F. Kennedy of Massachusetts had called the judge who had sentenced him. Kennedy reminded the judge of all the bad publicity he was getting for holding the famous Martin Luther King. Then they arranged bail.

Kennedy was running for president of the United States, and he wanted the African-American vote. He had invited King to dinner and to conferences, asking King to help him. So far, though, King hadn't given his support to either Kennedy, a Democrat, or Richard Nixon, the Republican candidate. He felt that both candidates were just trying to use African Americans to win the election.

After Kennedy arranged his release from jail, King told the press that the senator had taken a brave stand against the horrible treatment of African Americans in the South. That November, Kennedy narrowly won the election with the help of two-thirds of all African-American votes. President Kennedy appointed more than 40 African Americans to high positions in the government. However, he refused to push for a new civil rights bill because it would anger powerful white southern politicians.

A few months after Kennedy was elected, CORE began another form of demonstration called Freedom Rides. On the Freedom Rides, blacks and whites rode interstate buses together through the South. They wanted to call attention to segregated buses and bus stations throughout the South. Although the Supreme Court had outlawed this form of segregation in 1946 and 1960, nothing had really changed. In May 1961, a group of Freedom Riders boarded two buses in Washington, D.C., and headed for New Orleans. They had no idea how dangerous their ride would be.

Near Anniston, Alabama, an armed mob set one of the buses on fire. Passengers barely escaped before the bus exploded into flames. Freedom Riders on the second bus were beaten. When they reached Birmingham, Alabama, the police gave a gang of whites 15 minutes alone with the Freedom Riders. The riders never fought back, even when the mob beat them with lead pipes and baseball bats until they were bloody.

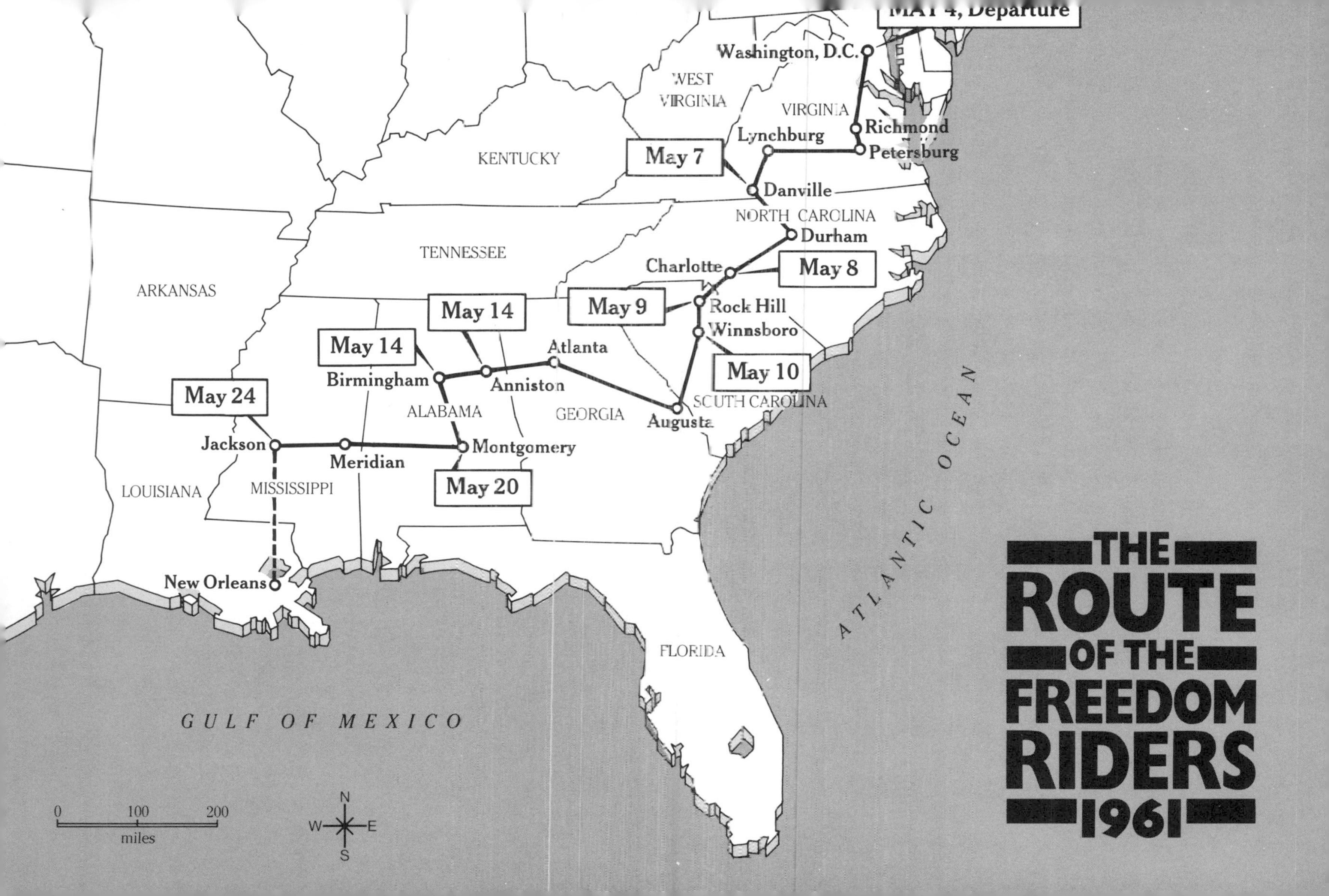

THE ROUTE OF THE FREEDOM RIDERS 1961

MAY 4, Departure
Washington, D.C.
Richmond
Petersburg
Lynchburg
Danville
May 7
Durham
May 8
Charlotte
Rock Hill
May 9
Winnsboro
May 10
Augusta
Atlanta
Anniston
May 14
Birmingham
May 14
Montgomery
May 20
Meridian
Jackson
May 24
New Orleans
WEST VIRGINIA
VIRGINIA
KENTUCKY
NORTH CAROLINA
TENNESSEE
SOUTH CAROLINA
GEORGIA
ALABAMA
MISSISSIPPI
ARKANSAS
LOUISIANA
FLORIDA
ATLANTIC OCEAN
GULF OF MEXICO
0 100 200
miles
N
W E
S

A few days later, another group headed out from Birmingham to Montgomery. As the riders filed off the bus in Montgomery, the station was deadly quiet. Suddenly hundreds of whites appeared with pipes and clubs, screaming, "Kill the niggers!" When King saw the brawl on TV he was furious that the riders were receiving no protection. He called Abernathy in Montgomery to tell him he was on his way.

Robert F. Kennedy, the president's brother and attorney general of the United States, begged King not to go. The government couldn't protect him, Robert Kennedy said. However, the day after King arrived in Montgomery, Robert Kennedy sent 400 federal marshals there. Alabama's governor, John Patterson, did nothing.

The following evening, King spoke to a mass meeting at Abernathy's church in Montgomery. Outside, a screaming mob of whites set fire to a car and threw rocks at the church windows. King and the others were trapped inside. Federal marshals held the mob back all night. Around dawn, Governor Patterson finally sent the Alabama National Guard and the state police to help break up the mob.

Robert Kennedy wanted the Freedom Riders to stop. The president was meeting with leaders of the Soviet Union, and he was embarrassed by the rides. The Freedom Riders voted to ride on, no matter what. King couldn't join them, however. He was still on probation. If he joined them, he would certainly be arrested and sent back to prison. He felt that he had to stay free in order to raise bail money for the Freedom Riders and the sit-in students who were being arrested.

Some of the riders were disappointed in King. One of them said, "I would rather have heard King say, 'I'm scared—that's why I'm not going.' I would have had greater respect for him if he had said that."

During the summer of 1961, more than 350 Freedom Riders were beaten and sent to jail. That September, Robert Kennedy ordered the Interstate Commerce Commission to enforce desegregation laws on buses and in stations. The Freedom Riders had won! That summer also saw victory for the sit-in protesters. Their protests brought about desegregation at lunch counters in more than 150 cities.

The Freedom Rides and sit-ins were aimed at changing or enforcing specific laws. In Albany, Georgia, a movement had started to try to change many different segregation laws at one time. In November 1961, Dr. William Anderson, president of the Albany Movement, asked King to speak at a rally being held there. The Albany Movement was made up of several groups that had come to demonstrate in that city. However, the groups were fighting among themselves over who should lead, and as a result, the demonstrations had come to a standstill.

After the rally, Anderson begged King to stay, and he agreed. The media rushed to Albany to cover King's latest demonstration. In December, King was arrested during a march. He vowed that he would stay in jail until city officials completely desegregated Albany. While he was in jail, the city council made a secret deal with some of the leaders in the African-American community. The council agreed to desegregate the bus and train stations, release all demonstrators, and allow African Americans to take their demands before a City Commission meeting. In return, blacks would stop their demonstrations.

The local African-American leaders agreed to the deal, and King was released from jail before he knew what had taken place. Then the city officials refused to integrate or meet with them. Outside of jail, King was no longer in a good position to make demands on the city. What's more, the media thought that he not only knew about the deal, but had approved it because he left jail. To make matters worse, King realized that jealousy and fighting among the civil rights groups had become worse since he arrived. They resented the attention the press gave him. This was especially true of SNCC, which had been operating there months before King came on the scene.

Martin Luther King, Jr., at the dinner table with his family.

Police Chief Laurie Pritchett seemed to outsmart King at every turn as he tried to gain some control of the situation in Albany. Pritchett sent demonstrators to jails in neighboring counties so that they could never fill the Albany jails. He used King's methods of nonviolence with the protesters, and he even gave King round-the-clock police protection

Finally, a federal judge banned demonstrations in Albany. King got himself arrested once again, hoping to force the city to negotiate. But the city officials set him free. With that, King realized that he had lost control of the Albany Movement. He left feeling devastated. At home, he spent time with his family and tried to sort out what went wrong.

King wasn't home much during this time. When he was, he tried to make up for the time he was gone. He played and joked with his children. While working in his study, he allowed them to come in with questions or to show him something they had made. "You know," King told a friend, "we adults are always so busy, we have so many things on our minds. . . . We tend to forget that they are trying to survive in a world they have to create for themselves."

Yoki was now six, and Marty was four. A new member of the family, Dexter Scott, would be one year old in January 1962. The Kings always tried to protect their children from the pain of segregation, just as their own parents had done. But one day, the time came when they could no longer protect Yoki.

Yoki had often begged her parents to take her to Funtown, a whites-only amusement park in Atlanta. They had never told her exactly why she couldn't go. One day, after seeing a commercial for Funtown on TV, she came running excitedly to her parents, eager to go.

Later, King remembered: "I have won some applause as a speaker, but my tongue twisted and my speech stammered seeking to explain to my six-year-old daughter why the public invitation on television didn't include her. . . . One of the most painful experiences I have ever faced was to see her tears. . . . I realized that at that moment the first dark cloud of inferiority had floated into her little mental sky."

The Kings had always taught Yoki to be proud of being black. Now they tried to help her overcome any bitter feelings she might have toward whites. They explained that words such as "cracker" were just as hurtful to whites as the word "nigger" was to her. They told her that there were many white people who were working to change the laws that kept her out of Funtown.

The segregationists, however, were determined that their segregated way of life wouldn't change. One symbol of this way of life was "Ole Miss," the all-white University of Mississippi in Oxford. In September 1962, a federal court ordered Ole Miss to admit James Meredith, a black U.S. Air Force veteran. The entire state went into an uproar.

On September 30, Meredith arrived in Oxford. He was taken straight to his campus dorm by 24 federal guards. Meanwhile, a mob of whites had gathered at the school's administration building, thinking that Meredith would go there first. More than 500 federal marshals stood in front of the entrance to protect the building. The mob screamed at the marshals, "Two-four-six-eight, we ain't gonna integrate!" Then they began throwing rocks and bottles, overturning cars, and smashing windows.

It wasn't long before the riot got out of control. At 10 P.M., federal troops were sent to the campus. Governor Ross Barnett promised President Kennedy that he would send highway patrolmen. Instead, the governor announced over the radio: "I call on Mississippi to keep the faith and courage. We will never surrender."

Throughout the night, several hundred troops fought back the rioting whites. By the time the violence was over, 200 people had been arrested, 160 marshals had been injured, and 2 people had been killed.

King was horrified and frustrated as he watched the Ole Miss riot on TV. To him, Mississippi's white leaders had treated the college integration like a Civil War battle—"a cause that was lost a hundred years ago." President Kennedy seemed to think that enrolling one black student would take care of school integration.

King was almost ready for another demonstration, even though he was still terribly depressed about Albany. He had learned important lessons from Albany. For one thing, he and his people had to be totally organized. He had also learned how valuable the media, especially TV, could be. More and more people were watching the news on TV to see films of events. If he were the preacher of a movement, the TV might well be his pulpit, King realized.

But the media needed a good reason to cover an event. In order to attract the media's attention, King knew that he would have to create a dramatic scene. He needed a villain who would treat peaceful demonstrators so unjustly that the public would be outraged. He also needed the support of brave ordinary people who would march for their rights, or there would be no demonstrations to cover. Furthermore, he had to have the support of the federal government. This time King would have to find a city that was so segregated and full of villains that the federal government would have to support his movement.

He decided on Birmingham, Alabama, "the most thoroughly segregated city in the United States."

THE EYES OF THE WORLD ARE ON BIRMINGHAM

"Once on a summer day, a dream came true. The city of Birmingham discovered a conscience."

MARTIN LUTHER KING, JR.

Birmingham was so segregated that city officials had banned a book containing pictures of black and white rabbits. In addition, the city had two perfect villains. Birmingham's public safety commissioner, Eugene Connor, was a well-known racist. "Bull" Connor, as he was called, was in charge of the police force. He promised that as long as he was commissioner, "the niggers and white folks ain't gon' segregate together." Before he let that happen, "blood would run in the streets." The governor of Alabama, George Wallace, was nearly as opposed to integration as Connor was. Wallace had won the

1962 governor's race by vowing to "stand in the schoolhouse door" rather than integrate Alabama schools.

King felt that Birmingham was the perfect city for the next SCLC demonstrations. He had two reasons for going there. The first was to desegregate the city. The second was to pressure President Kennedy into pushing another civil rights bill through Congress. King planned to present the city with the SCLC's demands. When these demands were rejected, his people would demonstrate. Marches were against city laws, so demonstrators would be arrested. King's plan was to fill the jails. He himself would go to jail. The media would pay plenty of attention to a whole city of African Americans who were willing to go to jail for their rights. King also figured that Connor was bound to do something cruel and outrageous in front of the TV cameras. Then the country would see the shocking conditions in Birmingham and demand that the laws be changed.

Before he did anything, however, King made sure that his "army" knew how dangerous demonstrating could be. "I have to tell you that in my judgment, some of the people sitting here today will not come back alive from this [protest]. And I want you to think about it," he told a hushed audience at one meeting.

Demonstrators also went through nonviolence training. During training, SCLC members playacted real situations that the demonstrators might run into. Trainers shouted and cursed at the demonstrators. They beat and spit on them. The demonstrators learned how to deal with this abuse without fighting back. When they were ready to march, King told them, "Make going to jail your badge of honor."

In April 1963, the SCLC began its protests. It demanded that Birmingham open up the lunch counters, rest rooms, and drinking fountains in its downtown stores to African Americans. It also wanted African Americans to be hired in local businesses. The city refused.

Within a few days, hundreds of African-American protesters had marched peacefully and gone to jail. Then King and Abernathy were arrested. This was the 13th time King had been arrested for protesting. He and Abernathy usually marched together and were often put into the same cell. This time, however, he was thrown into solitary confinement where he was all alone in a small dark room.

This was harsh punishment for such a minor crime. King wasn't allowed to speak with anyone, not even a lawyer. He didn't know what was going on. He didn't even know what time it was. Was "Ab" all right? Were the people marching? Had anyone been hurt? Not knowing these things made King depressed and nervous.

The next day King's jailers were kinder to him. They allowed him to talk to Coretta, who had just given birth to their fourth child—Bernice Albertine. Coretta told Martin why he was being treated better. She had called President Kennedy, who promised to find out why King had been placed in solitary confinement. As soon as Kennedy called, the city officials began treating King better.

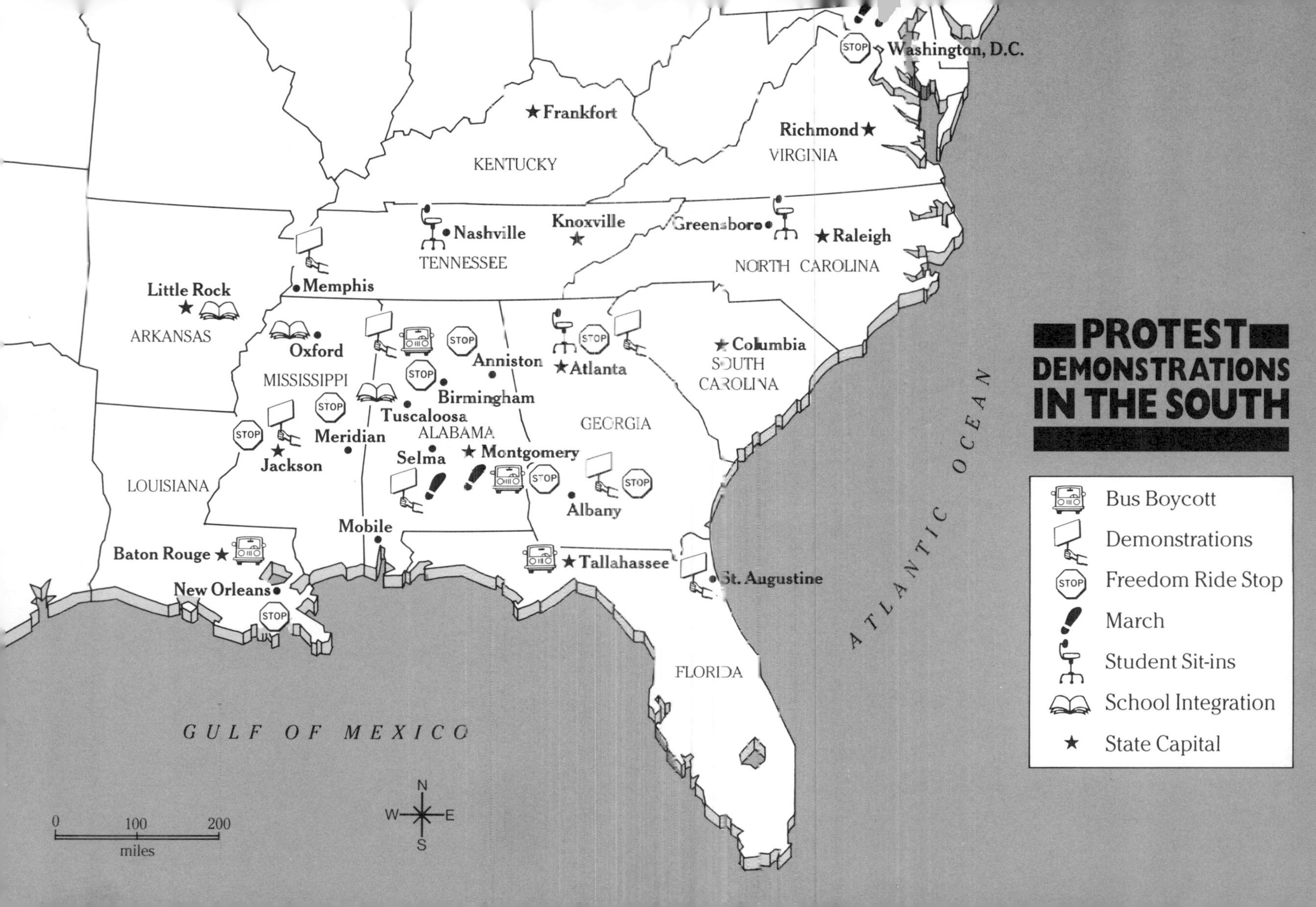
PROTEST DEMONSTRATIONS IN THE SOUTH
Bus Boycott
Demonstrations
Freedom Ride Stop
March
Student Sit-ins
School Integration
State Capital
Washington, D.C.
STOP
Frankfort
Richmond
VIRGINIA
KENTUCKY
Knoxville
Greensboro
Nashville
Raleigh
TENNESSEE
NORTH CAROLINA
Memphis
Little Rock
ARKANSAS
Oxford
MISSISSIPPI
Anniston
Atlanta
Columbia
SOUTH CAROLINA
Birmingham
Tuscaloosa
ALABAMA
GEORGIA
Meridian
Jackson
Selma
Montgomery
LOUISIANA
Albany
Mobile
Baton Rouge
Tallahassee
New Orleans
St. Augustine
ATLANTIC OCEAN
FLORIDA
GULF OF MEXICO
N
W
E
S
0
100
200
miles

One afternoon King's attorneys left a newspaper in his cell. It had printed a letter to King that had been written by eight respected white clergymen from Alabama. The clergymen criticized King, saying he was an outsider who should never have brought his movement to Birmingham. They wrote that he should have waited for a better time to protest. King decided to answer them with a letter of his own.

Since King wasn't allowed to have any writing materials in his cell, his lawyers sneaked a pen to him. He wrote the letter on toilet paper and on the edges of newspapers. This letter was smuggled out of the jail page by page by his lawyers. King's aides sent out nearly a million copies of this letter to churches, magazines, and politicians. The "Letter from a Birmingham Jail" became the bible of the protest movement.

In his letter King told the eight clergymen that he was not an outsider. "I am in Birmingham because injustice is here," he wrote. "Injustice anywhere is a threat to justice everywhere." He noticed that the clergymen thought the demonstrations in Birmingham were shameful, but they didn't seem to be concerned "for the conditions that brought about the demonstrations."

King then angrily attacked the ministers for wanting African Americans to wait for a better time to fight for their rights.

> For years now I have heard the word "Wait!"... This "Wait" has almost always meant "Never."... We have waited for more than 340 years for our constitutional and God-given rights. The nations of Asia and Africa are moving with jetlike speed toward gaining political independence, but we still creep at horse-and-buggy pace toward gaining of a cup of coffee at a lunch counter. Perhaps it is easy for those who have never felt the stinging darts of segregation to say, "Wait." But when you have seen vicious mobs lynch your mothers and fathers at will... when you have seen hate-filled policemen curse, kick, and even kill

your black brothers and sisters; when you see the vast majority of your twenty million Negro brothers smothering in an airtight cage of poverty in the midst of [a rich] society...when you are humiliated day in and day out by nagging signs reading "white" and "colored"...when you are forever fighting a degenerating sense of "nobodiness"—then you will understand why we find it difficult to wait.

Dr. King warned that if whites did not change peacefully, there were other blacks who were ready to use violent means to gain their rights. They were bitter and frustrated and had lost faith in the United States. Some of them were members of black nationalist groups who wanted to form a separate African-American nation within the United States or in Africa.

"Oppressed people cannot remain oppressed forever," King warned. "The Negro has many pent-up resentments and...frustrations. And he must release them....If [they] are not released in nonviolent ways, they will seek expression through violence; this is not a threat, but a fact of history.

King was fed up with whites who were wishy-washy about taking a stand on civil rights. "I have watched white churchmen stand on the sideline," he wrote. "The Negro's great stumbling block in his stride toward freedom is not the White Citizens Counciler or the Ku Klux Klanner, but the white moderate, who is more devoted to 'order' than to justice....I should have realized that few members of the oppressor race can understand the yearnings of the oppressed race."

A few days after the letter had been circulated, King and Abernathy were released from jail. But the movement had come to a standstill. It was running out of people to demonstrate. One of King's aides suggested letting college and high-school students march.

When the students showed up at the nonviolent workshops, so did their younger brothers and sisters. Hundreds of children,

Martin's wife, Coretta, was his firm ally during the troubled times in Birmingham.

some only six years old, demanded to march with the big kids. King was worried that the children might be hurt or even killed. But he also knew that "every day their minds were being hurt by segregation—and so were their spirits and souls." The children's crusade had begun.

On May 2, 1963, 1,000 children headed out toward downtown Birmingham singing and clapping. It made no difference to Bull Connor that the marchers were small children. He ordered his men to lock the "little niggers" up. One officer stopped an eight-year-old black girl and demanded to know what she wanted. "Fee-dom," she answered.

More than 950 children were arrested—so many that the police had to use school buses to haul them all to jail. King remembered the story of the woman who had refused a ride during the Montgomery bus boycott. She said that she was walking for her children and her grandchildren. Now "the children and grandchildren are doing it for themselves," King said proudly.

The next day, 1,000 more children showed up to march. This time Bull Connor had a surprise for them. Blocking the street stood a line of fire fighters holding water hoses. Beside them a group of policemen struggled to hold back snarling police dogs.

"Let 'em have it!" Connor hollered out. With that, the fire fighters turned on the hoses. The thick streams of water were so powerful that they tore off the marchers' clothes. The water swept some people into the street and sent others smashing into buildings and trees. Then the police dogs charged into the crowd while the police clubbed as many children as they could reach.

All across the nation, millions of people stared in disbelief at their TV sets and newspapers. President Kennedy said that what happened in Birmingham made him "sick." He didn't blame blacks for being tired of being asked to wait.

Two days later, thousands more gathered to march. When they reached the line of police and fire fighters, they knelt down to pray. Rev. Charles Billups, a young minister who was leading the march, stood up and spoke to the police. "We're not turning back. We haven't done anything wrong. All we want is our freedom. How do you feel doing these things?" Then Billups said, "Bring on your dogs. Beat us up. Turn on your hoses. We're not going to retreat." The marchers rose and began to move forward.

"Turn on the hoses!" yelled Bull Connor. But the policemen

The Birmingham Children's Crusade

The Birmingham children's crusade was the first time so many children of such a young age were arrested for protesting racism. On May 2, 1963, a thousand young people, some only six years old, began a peaceful protest against segregation in Birmingham, Alabama. The children took to the streets because many of their parents and older brothers and sisters had already been arrested for protesting. If the demonstration was to continue, new marchers would be needed. And, since the children did not have jobs, their arrest would not deprive their families of income. Older family members who were not arrested could still go to work and keep the household together. The children's crusade was a brilliant way of fighting racism. However, things became nasty on May 3, when Commissioner "Bull" Connor decided to attack the marchers with dogs and hoses.

A line of young blacks being escorted into Birmingham jail.

Young protesters in Birmingham are hosed, under orders of Police Commissioner "Bull" Connor

These girls were arrested during the protest and held in makeshift prisons like this one.

and the fire fighters just stood there. Again Connor ordered them to stop the marchers. Then the miracle of Birmingham happened. Connor's men, some of whom were crying, moved back to let the marchers pass. "I saw there, I felt there, for the first time... the power of nonviolence," King later wrote.

During these demonstrations, King had put into practice the Christian command to "turn the other cheek." When the marchers refused to strike back, the fire fighters and the policemen were forced to look at their own violent actions. They had to judge for themselves how right their beliefs were. When they did, many of them had a change of heart.

Finally, public outrage and pressure from President Kennedy became too great for Birmingham's city officials. They sat down with King to work out a way to integrate the city. Even though total integration was a long way off, Birmingham was now on its way to finding a better way of treating its African-American citizens.

11 THE DREAM

"At that moment it seemed as if the Kingdom of God had appeared. But it only lasted for a moment."

CORETTA SCOTT KING

On June 11, 1963, President Kennedy went on national TV to give a speech on civil rights and announce the new civil rights bill. King couldn't have been happier.

On the very night of the president's speech, white racists murdered Medgar Evers, a young black civil rights worker, in Jackson, Mississippi. In 1954, Evers had become the NAACP's first field director in Mississippi. A field director's job was a dangerous one—driving all over the state to encourage local people to join the NAACP. Evers had also worked on the

NAACP's legal battles in Mississippi. He had gathered evidence for the Emmett Till murder trial. He had helped James Meredith win his court battle to attend Ole Miss. Because of his work, Evers was an easy target for racist violence.

In spite of the president's message of understanding, the murder of Medgar Evers showed just how bitter racial hatred still was. It was clear that African Americans needed strong laws to overcome such blind hatred. Civil rights, religious, and labor leaders joined together for a huge march on the nation's capital to make sure Congress passed those laws.

The main organizer of this march was A. Philip Randolph. At 74, he was considered the father of the movement. For more than 50 years, he had been doing civil rights work. In 1925, he had founded the Brotherhood of Sleeping Car Porters, the first national black labor union. Sleeping-car porters waited on people who rode the railroad trains. Riding from one railroad station to another, Randolph tried to bring porters into the union and other movement operations.

Randolph had threatened to organize two mass protest marches to Washington, D.C., one in 1941 and another in 1947. He had called off both of them because two presidents of the United States had met his demands. He had now decided to stage another march for job training for blacks who were unemployed or earning lower wages than whites. After President Kennedy announced the civil rights bill, the goals of the march were expanded. These goals now included passage of the new bill, integration of public schools, and another bill to end job discrimination.

August 28, 1963, the day of the march, was hot. The organizers were hoping for 100,000 marchers to show up. That morning, King stood at the window of his hotel watching the crowds gather. He was worried because TV reporters said there were only about 25,000. But by midmorning, about 90,000 had arrived—and they were still coming.

By the time King joined the march, he was stunned. At least 250,000 people were marching. As many as 60,000 of them were white. People had come to the nation's capital that day to make a statement with their presence. They wanted the president of the United States and the world to know that they believed in equality for all and that it was time for African Americans to have theirs.

Slowly the huge crowd flowed around the long pool in front of the Lincoln Memorial. Musicians sang gospel hymns and folk songs while the audience waited for the speakers to begin. A. Philip Randolph was the first person to speak. "Fellow Americans," he began, "we are gathered here in the largest demonstration in the history of this nation. Let the nation and the world know the meaning of our numbers. We are not a pressure group, we are not an organization or a group of organizations, we are not a mob. We are the advance guard of a massive moral revolution for jobs and freedom."

John Lewis, chairperson of SNCC, gave a biting speech: "By the force of our demands, our determination and our number, we shall splinter the segregated South into a thousand pieces, and put them back together in the image of God and democracy."

King was the last speaker. It was three o'clock, and everyone was beginning to get restless. When Randolph introduced him as "the moral leader of the nation," the crowd clapped and shouted, "King! King! King!" He was the one they'd been waiting to hear. They were all attention now.

Martin Luther King, Jr., stood before the people, beneath the memorial of Abraham Lincoln, the president who had given African Americans their freedom. He had prepared his speech carefully.

> Fivescore years ago, a great American, in whose symbolic shadow we stand today, signed the Emancipation Proclamation [which freed the slaves].... But one hundred years later, the Negro still is not free; one hundred years later, the life of the Negro is still sadly crippled by the manacles of segregation and the chains of discrimination....
>
> ...There will be neither rest nor tranquility in America until the Negro is granted his citizenship rights. The whirlwinds of the revolt will continue to shake the foundations of our nation until the bright day of justice emerges.... We can never be satisfied as long as the Negro is the victim of the unspeakable horrors of police brutality.... We can never be satisfied as long as our children are stripped of their selfhood and robbed of their dignity.... We cannot be satisfied as long as the Negro in Mississippi cannot vote and a Negro in New York believes he has nothing for which to vote....

As King spoke, the huge audience swayed and shouted in rhythm with him. He looked out over a sea of upturned faces, united by an idea of love and the hope of equality. Suddenly he put down his notes and spoke from his heart.

> So I say to you today, my friends, that even though we face the difficulties of today and tomorrow, I still have a dream. It is a dream deeply rooted in the American dream that one day this nation will rise up and live out the true meaning of its creed—"we hold these truths to be self-evident, that all men are created equal." I have a dream that one day on the red hills of Georgia, sons of former slaves and sons of former slave owners will be able to sit down together at the table of brotherhood. I have a dream that one day even the state of Mississippi, a state sweltering with the heat of injustice [and] oppression, will be transformed into an oasis of freedom and justice. I have a dream that my four little children will one day live in a nation where they will not be judged by the color of their skin but by the content of their character.

"I have a dream today!" King shouted, and the crowd went wild. "Dream some more," they shouted back. Beside him his aides responded, "Tell it, doctor!" "All right!" He continued:

> This is our hope. This is the faith that I go back to the South with. . . . With this faith we will be able to transform the jangling discords of our nation into a beautiful symphony of brotherhood. With this faith we will be able to work together, to pray together, to struggle together, to go to jail together, to stand up for freedom together, knowing that we will be free one day. This will be the day when all of God's children will be able to sing with new meaning—"my country 'tis of thee, sweet land of liberty, of thee I sing. Land where my fathers died, land of the pilgrim's pride; from every mountainside, let freedom ring." And if America is to be a great nation, this must become true. . . .

As the old-time preachers would say, the spirit was in him.

The March on Washington

The March on Washington, August 28, 1963, was the emotional high point of the civil rights movement. More than 250,000 people gathered in the city to stand up for racial equality. On that day, the leaders and groups that made up the movement acted together and showed the world a united front. Martin Luther King, Jr., spoke to the thousands of marchers on that summer afternoon, and before millions more who were watching on TV. His speech helped define the movement. The Lincoln Memorial was the perfect setting. More than 100 years earlier, Abraham Lincoln had taken on the fight to end slavery, proclaiming that it was "the eternal struggle between these two principles—right and wrong—throughout the world." Now King took his place in history alongside the man who had ended slavery. There was a new battle to be won: the battle for true equality.

Martin Luther King, Jr., addresses a spellbound audience at the high point of the 1963 March on Washington.

The crowd swells around the Lincoln Memorial (photo taken from a helicopter).

King's voice soared and became more powerful with every sentence. As the power of his own words gripped him and the people responded to him, his rich baritone trembled with emotion.

> So let freedom ring from the hilltops of New Hampshire...the mighty mountains of New York...the Alleghenies of Pennsylvania...the Rockies of Colorado...the slopes of California.... Let freedom ring from Stone Mountain of Georgia...from Lookout Mountain of Tennessee...from every hill and molehill of Mississippi. From every mountainside, let freedom ring. And when this happens and when we allow freedom to ring, when we let it ring from every village and every hamlet, from every state and every city, we will be able to speed up that day when all God's children...will be able to join hands and sing in the words of the old Negro spiritual: "Free at last. Free at last. Thank God Almighty, we are free at last!"

As King stepped down into Abernathy's arms, the crowd roared, crying and hugging one another. When he tried to leave, the people surged toward him. Their desire to be near him was so great that the other leaders had to form a circle around him to protect him.

That day blacks in the audience and all over the nation felt a stronger sense of unity. The 1963 March on Washington gave both blacks and whites a sense that a new day was here and anything was possible. Most Americans watching the March on Washington on their TVs had never seen any civil rights event like this one. Until then what they had seen was mostly pictures of protest demonstrations, beatings, and jailings. This time there was no violence, no hatred. There was only a glorious coming together of all kinds of people to express one hope—the hope for freedom. To the nation, Martin Luther King, Jr., symbolized that hope with his dream of equality.

Only 18 days later, the dream was shattered.

12 THE ROAD TO FREEDOM IS ROCKY

> *"If you want us to stop marching, make justice a reality. I don't mind saying ... I'm tired of marching for something that should've been mine at birth. ... I don't march because I like it. I march because I must."*
>
> MARTIN LUTHER KING, JR.

On September 15, 1963, King's brother A.D. called him from Birmingham with news of a terrible tragedy. A black church had just been bombed. It was Sunday, and 400 people had gathered there to worship. The bomb blew a hole in the back of the church, where children were putting on their choir robes. One 12-year-old girl stumbled out of the hole, blinded. Four other girls were killed. One was 11 years old, and the other three were 14.

King rushed to Birmingham. He felt sad and bitter, but at the little girls' funeral he tried to give the people hope. He told them that the girls "did not die in vain. God still has a way of [pulling] good out of evil. . . . The innocent blood of these little girls may . . . bring new light to this dark city."

In his heart, however, King wondered how anyone could feel such hatred that he or she would plant a bomb in a crowded church. Some African Americans felt that they should protect themselves with guns. But the father of Denise McNair, one of the dead girls, replied, "I'm not for that. What good would Denise have done with a machine gun in her hand?"

Real protection for African Americans wasn't guns but better laws. King was more determined than ever that Congress should pass the new civil rights bill. He kept putting pressure on Congress by writing magazine articles and making speeches. On November 22, 1963, he was in his bedroom at home packing for a speaking trip. The TV was on. Suddenly a voice interrupted the program with a special news bulletin. President Kennedy had been shot in Dallas, Texas.

Martin called Coretta. Together they sat on the bed and watched the news bulletin. In a short while the grim news came that the president was dead. Martin sat staring at the TV screen. "I don't think I'm going to live to reach forty," he said quietly.

"Oh, don't say that, Martin," cried Coretta.

"This is what is going to happen to me also. I keep telling you, this is a sick nation. And I don't think I can survive either." Coretta tried to think of something that would change her husband's mind. But she knew that he could be right. There was nothing she could say, so they just sat there together in silence like the rest of the country.

They watched as Vice President Lyndon B. Johnson was sworn in as the new president of the United States. What would Johnson do for civil rights? King wondered. Kennedy had become a strong fighter for civil rights during his short time as president. Some people, however, said it was King's pressure on Kennedy that had forced him to take a stand against injustice. Would Johnson respond to King, too?

On November 27, Johnson delivered his first speech to Congress. He said the new civil rights bill should go through immediately. Johnson's speech sounded encouraging to King. But as 1963 ended, Congress still had not passed the bill.

In January 1964, King appeared on the cover of *Time* magazine. Each year *Time* announced a "Man of the Year." This year it was King. He was the first African American to receive this honor. During the past year, he had traveled 275,000 miles and spent 20 hours a day working for the movement. By now he had earned more than 50 awards and honorary degrees.

The SCLC was now the second most popular African-American organization in the country, next to the NAACP. King knew that the SCLC could easily become a national organization. He also knew that this move would threaten leaders of the NAACP and other African-American groups, such as CORE and the National Urban League. He decided that to keep peace and unity in the movement, the SCLC would continue to be based in the South.

The next SCLC demonstration was planned for St. Augustine, Florida. Robert Hayling, a black dentist, had helped start a protest movement there in 1963. St. Augustine was segregated and violent, like Birmingham. The city's sheriff, L. O. Davis, had a special police force just to keep blacks "in line." Most of that force was made up of the Ku Klux Klan.

King and the SCLC began demonstrations in St. Augustine in May 1964. They demanded that the city desegregate all public places and hire black policemen and fire fighters. The city officials refused, and march after march ended in violence. During one demonstration, about 800 Klan members carrying clubs ripped into a line of marchers. Dr. Hayling said that it was hard for him to look at "the wounds and the split skulls and the broken noses and broken arms."

No matter what the protesters did, the officials refused to give in, and President Johnson refused to send any federal troops. King began to worry that St. Augustine would turn into another Albany. He didn't want to get stuck there, unable to attend to work in other places. Finally, the governor established a committee of blacks and whites to discuss the problems. This committee was hardly a victory for King, but it was enough for him to end the demonstrations there and leave.

It seemed that King had won a victory when Congress finally passed the 1964 Civil Rights Act. On July 2, King and other black leaders were invited to the White House to watch President Johnson sign this bill into law. It banned discrimination because of color, race, religion, or sex. Any institution or program that practiced discrimination could lose any federal funding it received. The bill established the Equal Employment Opportunity Commission to help everyone receive equal job opportunities. It also made Jim Crow segregation illegal. Furthermore, it gave the government the power to sue any school system that refused to desegregate. Even though the bill included all minorities, it gave the most protection to African Americans.

But King wasn't satisfied with the bill. It said nothing about segregated housing. It also didn't give the government the power to enforce laws against bad treatment of African Americans. And it didn't do enough about voting rights. Many people didn't understand why African Americans weren't satisfied with the bill.

During an interview, King replied angrily: "Why do white people seem to find it so difficult to understand that the Negro is sick and tired of [slowly receiving] those rights...which all others receive upon birth or entry in America? I never cease to wonder at... white society, assuming that they have the right to bargain with the Negro for his [or her] freedom."

King felt that achieving voting rights was the most important right African Americans could work for. In July 1964, the SCLC joined CORE and SNCC in Mississippi on a project called Freedom Summer. Freedom Summer was started to help blacks in Mississippi register so they could vote for president in the 1964 election. At that time in Mississippi, only about 5 percent of blacks who could vote were registered.

Eight hundred black and white college students from the North used their summer vacation to go to Mississippi and help register blacks. The students also started freedom schools to teach blacks reading and math. Most blacks in Mississippi had little schooling. They spent practically all of their time working in the fields.

The young people weren't always aware of how dangerous it was to do civil rights work in the backwoods of Mississippi. It was much more dangerous than marching in a city. No one would know if a young civil rights worker had been kidnapped on a dark, lonely road. On June 20, three were reported missing: James Chaney, a black man from Mississippi, and Andrew Goodman and Michael Schwerner, two white men from New York.

For years blacks had been disappearing in Mississippi. Few people except their friends and family had ever cared. Now it was different. Two whites were missing. More than 200 federal officers searched for them in the woods and in the rivers. The media reported on the search every day. Chaney, Goodman, and Schwerner were finally found—buried near Philadelphia, Mississippi. They had been shot to death. These three young men became heroes of the movement.

One of the results of the voting rights effort that Freedom Summer was the Mississippi Freedom Democratic Party (MFDP). The MFDP was made up of blacks and whites. They wanted to take the place of the all-white Democratic party that was representing Mississippi at the Democratic National Convention that August.

King worked hard to get the MFDP accepted by officials at the convention. He didn't know that President Johnson had promised the all-white group that the MFDP would be kept out. Johnson, a Democrat and a smart politician, wanted unity

Martin Luther King, Jr., holds pictures of three civil rights workers who were missing in Mississippi.

in his party and a quiet convention. He knew that Mississippi Democrats wouldn't put up with any blacks representing their state. He therefore approved a plan to admit two members of the MFDP. However, they would not officially represent Mississippi. The plan included passing a rule that groups representing Mississippi at future Democratic conventions would have to be integrated.

King urged the MFDP to take the offer. He felt that they were foolish to think they'd get more from politicians at this

time. But the MFDP disagreed. They had followed all the rules for becoming a legal party. They maintained that the all-white party wasn't legal because it didn't represent everyone who lived in Mississippi. The MFDP said no deal.

Fannie Lou Hamer, a poor Mississippi sharecropper, was one of the founders of the MFDP. She told TV reporters, "We didn't come all this way for... token rights, on the back row, the same as we got in Mississippi."

The MFDP was turned away from the convention that year. But because of them, 1964 was the last year a segregated group of representatives was accepted at the Democratic convention.

After the convention King traveled to every major city, urging blacks to vote for Johnson. Even though Johnson had made deals with white Mississippians behind the scenes, King was against Barry Goldwater, the Republican candidate. He reminded audiences that Goldwater had voted against the civil rights bill. He said Goldwater believed blacks were poor because they were lazy. On election day in November 1964, most blacks voted for Johnson, who won by a landslide victory over Goldwater.

At almost the same time, King was awarded the Nobel Peace Prize. The 35-year-old civil rights leader was then the youngest person, and only the third African American to receive the prize. In December he flew to Oslo, Norway, to claim the prize. He was introduced as a "champion of peace," someone who had "shown us that a struggle can be waged without violence." King wept as he walked onstage to get his prize. Nothing meant more to him than this special honor for being a peacemaker. In his speech he said that he accepted the Nobel Peace Prize for 22 million African Americans.

It had been a rocky road from Montgomery, Alabama, to Oslo, Norway—for Martin Luther King, Jr., and for everyone who had marched by his side. Now it was time for them to march once again—this time for the right to vote.

AN IDEA WHOSE TIME HAS COME

"I know you are asking today, 'How long will it take?' I come to say to you this afternoon, however difficult the moment, however frustrating the hour, it will not be long. . . . How long? Not long, because no lie can live forever."

MARTIN LUTHER KING, JR.

King wanted stronger voting rights laws for African Americans. He decided that Selma, Alabama, was a good place to have a demonstration for voting rights. In Selma, less than 1 percent of blacks who were old enough to vote were registered. The registration office was open only two days a month. Blacks who came to register were asked as many as 100 questions. Many of the questions couldn't be answered even by someone who had studied politics. Often the white officials themselves couldn't read the questions. If a black person forgot to cross a "t" on a form, he or she would be rejected.

When King arrived in January 1965, he found that many streets in the black section of Selma were still not paved. He learned that blacks on a nearby plantation had never seen U.S. money. They were paid with tokens and bought everything they needed at the plantation store. With the vote, King told blacks in Selma, they could change these terrible living conditions.

As soon as King arrived, so did the reporters. Selma's sheriff, James Clark, told reporters that blacks couldn't pass the registration tests because they weren't born smart enough. Clark had threatened blacks who tried to register and attacked SNCC workers who were helping them. King knew that Clark would attack demonstrators in front of TV crews covering the marches.

On January 18, King and a group of blacks marched to the courthouse to register. Sheriff Clark lined them up in the back alley to wait. There they would be away from the reporters. No one was registered that day. The following day, the marchers refused to go into the alley. Sheriff Clark became angry. He grabbed one marcher by the collar of her coat and shoved her roughly down the street. The next day the TV networks showed Clark pushing a black woman with one hand and holding a large club in the other.

King planned to be arrested and write another letter from jail. On February 1, he led 250 marchers and was jailed. Then 800 children, along with 100 adults, marched and were also arrested. TV news showed the children being led off to jail. The jails were packed. King's "Letter from a Selma Jail" said that there were more blacks in jail with him than there were blacks registered to vote in Selma.

While King was in jail, Malcolm X, a powerful black Muslim leader in the North, visited Selma. He had been invited there by SNCC to give a speech. Earlier in his life, Malcolm X had believed that whites were the devil. He no longer believed this. Now he felt that the "cause of brotherhood" was the only thing that could save the country.

But Malcolm X didn't believe in turning the other cheek if a white person slapped him. Many militant blacks were adopting Malcolm X's ways over King's. Reporters wrote that the movement was dividing into Martin's children and Malcolm's children.

After his speech, Malcolm X gave Coretta King a message for her husband. He wanted the nonviolent leader to know that he hadn't come to Selma to make it more difficult for him. He just wanted to let southerners know what the "alternative" to King's nonviolence was. Perhaps whites would then be more willing to listen to King.

Less than three weeks later, Malcolm X was gunned down in New York City.

On February 18, demonstrators in nearby Marion held a nighttime march, which was very dangerous. Suddenly the street lights went out. In the darkness, state troopers beat marchers brutally with clubs. When 26-year-old Jimmy Lee Jackson tried to protect his mother and grandfather, a trooper shot him in the stomach. Jackson died a week later. King, who was now out of jail, delivered a eulogy at the funeral.

Some demonstrators were so angry that they wanted to carry Jackson's body to Governor George Wallace in Montgomery, the state capital. Instead, the SCLC decided to hold a march from Selma to Montgomery, 50 miles away. SNCC didn't want this march. It was too dangerous, and there had been too many deaths already. But King felt that the four-day march would draw the media's attention.

The march was scheduled for Sunday, March 7, 1965. That day about 525 people started out for Highway 80, which led to Montgomery. As they crossed the Edmund Pettus Bridge, they saw three rows of state troopers blocking the four-lane highway. The troopers plowed into the screaming demonstrators, knocking them down, stomping on them, and clubbing their heads. Then they fired tear gas. Choking and crying, the marchers tried to get away through the blinding smoke. Some of the

Malcolm X holds up a newspaper during a Black Muslim rally in New York City.

troopers followed them on horses. They rode through the crowds beating people until they fell unconscious and bleeding. The TV stations interrupted their regular programs to show pictures of what they called Bloody Sunday.

King was in Atlanta that day giving a sermon at the Ebenezer Baptist Church. He immediately sent telegrams to people all over the country asking them to join him for a second march on Tuesday. For most of them this was a call they couldn't refuse. Overnight, 400 people went to Selma to stand with King.

On Tuesday morning, the march was banned. But King decided to go ahead anyway. Too many had come too far to march with him. But when the 1,500 marchers reached the bridge, the troopers were waiting again. King didn't have the law to support him, and he didn't want to put the marchers in danger again. He turned back.

This made many SNCC leaders furious. Some of the ministers who had come also felt betrayed by King's decision to turn around. However, King might have been right to try to protect the marchers. The local white racists were in an ugly mood. That night they clubbed three clergymen. A northern white minister, James Reeb, died from this beating two days later. After Reeb's death, President Johnson received phone calls from all over the country demanding that he send federal troops to Selma.

On Monday, March 15, King conducted a memorial service for Reeb in front of the Selma courthouse. That night President Johnson announced on TV that he had sent a new voting rights bill to Congress. He told the American public that the civil rights movement was everyone's cause. Everyone—black and white—had to overcome prejudice and injustice. "And we shall overcome!" he added. By the end of Johnson's speech, King was crying.

There was another victory—a judge had approved the march. On Sunday, March 21, King led more than 3,000 people toward Highway 80. Black and white people from all over the country had come to march to Montgomery: priests, ministers, nuns, rabbis, students, politicians, and movie stars.

White bigots were outraged at this display of integration and protest. They lined the roads shouting, "Nigger lovers!" Small white children pointed toy guns at the white marchers and yelled, "White nigger!"

Along the way, the marchers passed small African-American communities. They walked by broken-down churches and a school that was propped up with bricks. They saw shacks with holes in the walls. Poor blacks who lived in the area came to watch the marchers pass by. One old man with a cane came

Martin Luther King, Jr., leads the march to Montgomery.

limping across a field to meet King. "I just wanted to walk one mile with y'all," he told King.

The march took five days. King didn't march the whole way, though. He had to keep up a busy schedule, making speeches and raising money for the movement. But he was there on Thursday, March 25, to lead some 25,000 people through Montgomery. Waving flags and cheering, the marchers moved past the Dexter Avenue Baptist Church, King's first church. For King, the movement had come full circle. It had all started at Dexter 10 years before, with the bus boycott. With him now marched Rosa Parks, who had sparked the boycott and the movement.

Finally they reached the capitol building. Governor George Wallace peeked through the blinds of his office window at the huge crowd, but he refused to come out. Before national TV cameras, King cried out: "They told us we wouldn't get here. . . . but all the world today knows that we are here and that we are standing before the forces of power in the state of Alabama saying, 'We ain't goin' let nobody turn us around.'... Like an idea whose time has come, not even the marching of mighty armies can halt us. We are moving to the land of freedom!"

The Selma march was perhaps King's greatest moment as a leader. Before, hundreds of thousands of Americans had watched his marches at home on their TV sets. This time blacks and whites from all over the country actually went to Selma and marched together with him.

On August 6, King watched President Johnson sign the Voting Rights Act of 1965 into law. Without the Selma demonstrations and the great march, it might have taken Congress years to pass this law. The law outlawed tests used to disqualify blacks from registering in seven southern states. It also allowed the federal government to send officials there to register blacks if necessary, and to oversee federal elections there. Poll taxes, another hindrance to black voters, had already been banned in federal elections by the 24th Amendment to the U.S. Constitution. However, the state poll taxes were still legal, and this new law did not do away with them. Instead, it ordered the federal government to sue the four states where these poll taxes were still legal.

The major voting barriers to southern blacks were removed by the Voting Rights Act. By the following summer, the number of registered blacks in Dallas County, where Selma was located, had risen from 333 to 9,000. Within a few years the city council, police force, and schools in Selma were integrated. Sheriff Jim Clark was voted out of office. Bull Connor in Birmingham was also voted out. Other southern officials, such as Governor Wallace, stayed in office for several more terms. But they had to change the way they treated and spoke about blacks in order to win black votes.

King believed that having the power to vote would improve living conditions for African Americans. He was right.

14 ANGER AND DIVISION

> *"We have flown the air like birds, and swum the sea like fishes, but we have not learned the simple act of walking the earth like brothers."*
>
> MARTIN LUTHER KING, JR.

King was becoming disturbed by the voices of African Americans who had grown tired of nonviolent protest. These blacks felt that it was time to stop asking for their rights from whites. They wanted to take what was theirs. They were angry at having to wait for laws to be enforced, angry at how long it was taking for things to change.

Black anger was exploding all across the United States. In August 1965, a violent race riot tore apart Watts, a black section in Los Angeles, California. For six days, blacks there burned buildings and looted stores, destroying property worth $46 mil-

Troops called out to stem the rioting pass by some of the residents.

lion. By the time it was over, 34 people had been killed, 900 had been injured, and around 4,000 had been arrested.

King flew to Watts immediately and walked through the streets. He noted that most of the buildings that had been destroyed were those that charged high prices or took advantage of blacks. Black-owned businesses, as well as schools and libraries, had been left untouched. King learned some of the reasons for the anger in Watts. Watts was four times as crowded as the rest of Los Angeles. Many of its citizens were forced to live in run-down housing developments. Thirty percent of blacks there had no jobs.

For some time now, King had been concerned that the spring of anger blacks felt was wound tighter in the big cities—especially those in the North. Most blacks in these cities lived in segregated, run-down neighborhoods called ghettos. The rents in these ghettos were often higher than those in white sections. So were the prices of food and other goods. Blacks were forced to pay these higher prices because they weren't allowed to live anywhere else and often couldn't afford cars to drive to cheaper stores. Discrimination also kept blacks from holding good jobs. Between high prices and low-paying jobs, city blacks were often caught in a cycle of poverty.

King decided to take his nonviolent movement north to Chicago. In January 1966, King, the SCLC, and black leaders in Chicago formed the Chicago Freedom Movement. King moved into an apartment in a black section of Chicago called Slumdale.

King wanted to organize blacks in Chicago into a "Slum Union" that would be able to operate after the SCLC left. He asked everyone—from church leaders to street gangs—for money and help. He met with Mayor Richard Daley, who maintained that Chicago wasn't responsible for poverty in the ghettos. Poverty had been brought to this city by poor blacks from the South, Daley said.

Six months later, King interrupted his Chicago movement to return to the South. James Meredith, who had integrated Ole Miss four years earlier, had been shot and wounded. Meredith had been on a one-man march across Mississippi to encourage blacks to register. King met with Floyd McKissick, the new national director of CORE, and Stokely Carmichael, the new chairperson of SNCC. They decided that their organizations would continue Meredith's march for him. Meredith later joined them by car.

McKissick and Carmichael represented the growing number of militant blacks in the movement. Carmichael felt that blacks should seize power in places where there were more blacks than whites. He admired King, but he and McKissick were moving away from the SCLC's nonviolent method of protest. They also thought the Meredith march should be an all-black protest. When King threatened to leave unless the march was nonviolent and integrated, the young leaders gave in to his wishes.

One night Carmichael was arrested while trying to set up tents in a black school yard for the marchers to sleep in. When he was released, he spoke at a SNCC rally. "This is the twenty-seventh time I've been arrested. I ain't going to jail no more!" he screamed at the hundreds of people who had gathered. Blacks had been demanding freedom for six years and had gotten nothing, he declared. "What we gonna start saying now is black power!"

The crowd took up the cry of "BLACK POWER!" Carmichael's aides called out, "What do you want?" "BLACK POWER!" came the response.

"What do you want? Say it again!"

"BLACK POWER! BLACK POWER! BLACK POWER!"

King and other, older leaders were totally against using this term. It sounded as if those who used it were in favor of violence. When King led the march into Jackson, Mississippi, he considered it to be a victory for nonviolence. But it was the cry of "Black Power!" that the country remembered.

After the march, King returned to Chicago with his family. Riots broke out in Slumdale in July. For two days and nights, King drove around trying to calm down rioters. He finally talked Mayor Daley into doing something. Daley set up 10 portable swimming pools in the ghetto. He attached sprinklers to the fire hydrants so that children could play under the water.

Later, King held marches in white middle-class neighborhoods. Thousands of whites who lived there gathered and screamed, "Hate! Hate! Hate!" and "We hate niggers! Kill the niggers!" They smashed the marchers' cars and hurled bricks and bottles at them. One brick hit King in the head. He had never seen such hatred in his life.

Daley was horrified at the attention King was getting from the media. Finally, he and the city officials met with King and his people. They came up with an agreement that was supposed to change the way city agencies, as well as banks and landlords, treated blacks. However, they had set no time limit for when certain changes should be made. Local leaders were angry when King accepted the agreement and called off further demonstrations. But King wanted to leave Chicago.

One of the programs he started before he left was Operation Breadbasket. Jesse Jackson, a new SCLC staff member, ran the program. Operation Breadbasket boycotted stores that sold to blacks but refused to hire them. The boycotts were successful in forcing stores to hire blacks.

Except for Operation Breadbasket, many people thought King's efforts in the North had failed. To King, Chicago felt like a northern Albany. In spite of his work in Chicago, blacks had rioted in 39 cities that spring. The more King thought about what he should do next, the more depressed he became.

More and more, King was also bothered by the Vietnam War. Vietnam was a small country in Southeast Asia. In 1954, it had been divided into two parts—North Vietnam and South Vietnam. North Vietnam was controlled by Communists, and South Vietnam was supported by the United States. An international agreement had called for free elections to unite the country. The United States was afraid the Communists might win, so it supported the leaders in South Vietnam. No free election was held, and soon a bloody civil war raged between North Vietnam and South Vietnam. Many governments and individual citizens felt that the United States was to blame for starting this civil war.

President Johnson had steadily increased U.S. involvement in the war. By June 1965, there were 75,000 soldiers in Vietnam, three times more than President Kennedy had sent. To keep down objections, Johnson didn't reveal the actual number of men and dollars being sent to Vietnam.

King felt that he had a responsibility to speak out against this war. He hated the killing and injuring of human beings. He was afraid of the possibility of nuclear war, too. He felt that it was "worthless to talk about integrating if there is no world to integrate in."

In August, King expressed his objections to the war on a national TV show. He offered to go to Vietnam and try to bring peace. President Johnson was furious. Who did King think he was? The black leader should fight for black rights and keep out of government business that didn't concern him. Before that TV show, King could call the president directly on the phone. Overnight, that changed.

By the fall of 1966, the number of soldiers fighting in Vietnam had risen to 350,000. In early 1967, King wrote a book, *Where Do We Go From Here?* In it he wrote that the U.S. government was spending about $332,000 for every enemy it killed in Vietnam. At the same time, it was spending only about $53 on each person in its antipoverty programs. He felt that the money being spent on the war in Vietnam should be spent to relieve poverty at home.

President Johnson had already declared a War on Poverty program in the United States. He had established programs to solve housing problems and to guarantee health care to the poor and the elderly. He had also raised the minimum wage and pushed through a $4 billion bill for education. These programs would benefit millions of Americans, including many African Americans.

However, as Johnson spent more money on the Vietnam War, he cut back on these programs. Objections to these cutbacks were adding to the growing movement against the war. Huge protest rallies were held. Young men refused to be drafted into the army. The war was tearing the United States apart.

In 1967, the country spent $20 billion on the war, while hundreds of poverty-stricken ghettos rocked with riots that summer. The worst riots were in Boston, Cincinnati, Newark, and Detroit. For days, sections of these cities burned while blacks and police shot at each other in the streets. Johnson sent tanks and paratroopers into Detroit to stop the rioting. On TV, he scolded blacks for not obeying the law. But he never mentioned the terrible conditions they lived in that had caused them to riot.

King was angry that the U.S. government was sending young black men "8,000 miles away to guarantee liberties in Southeast

Thousands gather in Washington in this SNCC protest against U.S. involvement in Vietnam.

Asia which they had not found in Southwest Georgia and East Harlem."

The war was one issue that Martin Luther King, Jr., and Stokely Carmichael agreed on. Carmichael pointed out that more blacks were being sent to fight and die in Vietnam than whites, which made it a white racist war. "Hell, no, we won't go! . . . Ain't no Vietcong ever called me a nigger," he shouted to cheering antiwar crowds. "If I'm going to do any fighting it's gonna be right here at home."

But other civil rights leaders did not approve of King's views. They told King that his stand on the war would cause the movement to lose support from the president. The war was one more thing that was tearing the movement apart. No matter whose support he lost, however, King felt too strongly about the war to keep silent. It was more important for him to do what he believed was right than to have praise. But what would that mean for the movement?

THE PROMISED LAND

"For years I labored with the idea of reforming the existing institutions of the South, a little change here, a little change there. Now I feel quite differently. I think you've got to have a reconstruction of the entire society, a revolution of values."

MARTIN LUTHER KING, JR.

King felt that a major change had to take place in the United States. He believed that the United States had taken advantage of many of its citizens—of all races. King felt that blacks had been treated the worst but that they weren't the only victims. He wanted to unite all the people in the country who had been left out of the American dream—red and yellow, black and white. He called his idea the Poor People's Campaign.

King planned to bring thousands of poor people from all over the country to set up a city in Washington, D.C. After a huge rally, they would begin nonviolent demonstrations and fill the jails for three months or longer. During this time, the SCLC would begin boycotts all over the nation. Then businesses would force Congress to meet King's demands for the poor. King knew it would be a huge job. "Before we have mobilized [organized] one city at a time, now we are mobilizing a nation," he said.

When King announced his plan for the Poor People's Campaign in December 1967, very few people supported him. SCLC leaders were already angry with him because his antiwar stand had caused contributions to the SCLC to drop. The NAACP leaders were afraid that his poor people's "army" would cause a riot in Washington. Just like the eight clergymen of Alabama, they cried that King had gone too far. They felt that he should wait for a better time. At the same time, black militants like Stokely Carmichael were accusing King of not having gone far enough.

President Johnson had cut King off completely. Johnson felt that he had done more for blacks than any other president had done. He was angry that King wasn't satisfied. The Federal Bureau of Investigation (FBI) was trying to turn everyone against the powerful black leader. The FBI had considered King to be dangerous ever since he began urging blacks to demand their rights. They tried to brand him a Communist. They tapped his home phones and those of his friends. They put recording devices in all the hotel rooms in which he stayed. King and his staff were convinced that Johnson was working with the FBI to try to halt the Poor People's Campaign.

Not all of King's staff were behind his Poor People's Campaign. How could anyone, even King, unite all the different poor people—Puerto Ricans, Native Americans, Asian Americans, whites, blacks, and others? If it failed, King would lose the respect of many people. Then what would happen to the movement?

King's staff estimated that it would cost anywhere from $400,000 to $1 million to create a poor people's city in the capital. Where would the money come from? The project was scheduled for April 1968. It was now February. How could they get everything done in time?

King needed his staff's support and was crushed when they kept bringing him nothing but doubts. Sometimes he felt that everything he was doing was too much for one man to do. On top of this, he had been asked to help black garbage collectors who were on strike in Memphis, Tennessee. He felt that he had to help them.

The garbage collectors had asked for decent wages and for the right to form a union. The white city government had refused, so the workers had gone on strike. King felt that if their strike was successful, it would help his march on Washington. On March 28, he led the garbage collectors in a march that broke out into a riot.

Afterward, King was full of guilt over the violence that had occurred. He had to lead another march, a successful one. The night before the next march, King was too depressed to give a rally speech, so he sent Abernathy to take his place. But his friend called to tell him that a crowd of 2,000 people were waiting for him. King felt that he couldn't disappoint them.

At the meeting place, he told the audience that the world was all messed up and the nation was sick. He recalled the time he was stabbed and said that he was glad he had lived to see so many victories in the movement.

"We've got some difficult days ahead," he continued. "But it doesn't matter with me now. Because I've been to the mountaintop. And I don't mind. Like anybody, I would like to live a long life.... But I'm not concerned about that now. I just want to do God's will. And He's allowed me to go up to the mountain. And I've looked over. And I've seen the Promised Land. And I may not get there with you. But I want you to know tonight that we as a people will get to the Promised Land."

Between each sentence, people applauded and cried out, "Oh, yes!" "Go ahead." "Yes, doctor!" "Tell it!"

Jesse Jackson and Ralph Abernathy on the balcony with Dr. King, hours before King is killed there.

"And I'm happy tonight," King told them. "I'm not worried about anything. I'm not fearing any man. Mine eyes have seen the glory of the coming of the Lord."

King's staff was concerned with how much he talked about dying. King believed he would someday be killed. Sometimes it got to him, wondering when it would happen. By 1968, the FBI had uncovered 50 threats on King's life. In spite of danger, King wouldn't allow anyone around him to carry a gun because that went against everything he stood for.

The next morning King's spirits had lifted. He and his staff made the final plans for the march that would be held the following Monday. At six o'clock, King stepped out onto the hotel balcony to wait for Abernathy to finish dressing. They were going to have dinner with a local minister.

Suddenly a shot rang out. A bullet tore through the right side of King's face and knocked him backward with its force. He crumpled to the floor holding his throat.

Within minutes, swarms of police had appeared, and an ambulance arrived. Abernathy rode in the ambulance, refusing to leave his friend. In the hospital doctors worked on King, but it was no use. At 7:05 on April 4, 1968, Martin Luther King, Jr., was pronounced dead. He was only 39 years old.

Abernathy gave the news to the three staff members who had been waiting in the hall. Months earlier, King had stood up in an SCLC meeting and declared that Abernathy would take his place if anything happened to him. At that time, the room was hushed in painful silence. Abernathy had said, "I do not look forward to filling the shoes of Martin Luther King, Jr. I don't think anyone can." Now one of the men reminded Abernathy of King's command.

Newspapers called King's murder a national disaster. Stokely Carmichael raged, "When white America killed Dr. King, she declared war on us. . . . Get your gun!" Angry blacks rioted in more than 100 cities across the country.

At least one peaceful march occurred. On April 8, Rev. Abernathy and Coretta King, along with three of her children, led 19,000 people silently through the streets of Memphis. The city agreed to recognize the garbage collectors' union and to raise their wages. The strike ended eight days later.

In Atlanta, more than 1,200 people filed past Martin Luther King, Jr.'s casket each hour to pay their last respects. Daddy King was beside himself with grief. He reached into his son's casket. "M.L.! Answer me, M.L.!" he cried. "He never hated anybody," Daddy King sobbed.

On April 9, the Ebenezer Baptist Church was packed with 800 civil rights leaders, SCLC staff, movie stars who had marched with King, and friends and family. Outside 60,000 to 100,000 people stood listening to the service over loudspeakers. Abernathy led the services: "We gather here this morning in one of the darkest hours in the history of the black people of this nation, in one of the darkest hours in the history of mankind."

Coretta King asked that a tape of one of her husband's sermons be played. It was one King had preached in Ebenezer only two months earlier. Once more his rich voice echoed through

A mule cart bears the body of Martin Luther King, Jr., through Memphis on April 9, 1968.

the church where he had grown up, where he had preached his very first sermon.

> Every now and then I think about my own death, and I think about my own funeral.... I ask myself, "What is it that I would want said?" And I leave the words to you this morning. If any of you are around when I have to meet my day, I don't want a long funeral. And if you get somebody to deliver the eulogy, tell them not to talk too long.... Tell them not to mention that I have a Nobel Peace Prize, that isn't important.... I'd like somebody to mention that day, that Martin Luther King, Jr., tried to give his life serving others. I'd like for somebody to say that day, that Martin Luther King, Jr., tried to love somebody. I want you to say that day that I tried to be right on the war question... that I did try to feed the hungry... that I tried to love and serve humanity.... Say I was a drum major for justice; say that I was a drum major for peace; I was a drum major for righteousness. And all of the other shallow things will not matter. I won't have any money to leave behind. I won't have the fine and luxurious things of life to leave behind. But I just want to leave a committed life behind.

King's casket was carried to his grave on a mule cart to symbolize the closeness he felt with poor people. One hundred and twenty million people watched Martin Luther King, Jr.'s last march on their TV sets. Fifty thousand marched along behind him.

At the cemetery, Abernathy declared, "The grave is too narrow for his soul." On his tombstone was written:

FREE AT LAST, FREE AT LAST
THANK GOD ALMIGHTY
I'M FREE AT LAST

EPILOGUE: HE TRIED TO LOVE SOMEBODY

"There is nothing in all the world greater than freedom. It is worth paying for. . . . If physical death is the price that some must pay to free their children from a permanent life of psychological death, then nothing could be more honorable."

MARTIN LUTHER KING, JR.

For 12 years Martin Luther King, Jr., led one of the most important American movements for social change in the 20th century. That movement brought about more positive changes in the law for African Americans than had occurred in all the other years they had lived in the United States. Many thought the civil rights movement had died with King. In fact, change still took place, but in different ways.

However, as Abernathy said, no one could fill the shoes of Martin Luther King, Jr.

For years most blacks, as well as whites, had accepted inequality without question. King changed all that. He showed African Americans that it wasn't their fault that they were being treated badly. He gave them a sense of self-worth, which they needed before they could demand their rights. He also realized that it wasn't enough for them to be able to sit down at a lunch counter if they had no money with which to buy food. He knew that until everyone—no matter what race—had equal opportunities for a better life, no person or race would be free.

To continue King's work, the Martin Luther King, Jr., Center for Nonviolent Studies was established. The center, located in Atlanta, Georgia, was also set up to house King's papers, which included books and thousands of speeches, sermons, articles, and letters.

In 1983, Congress made King's birthday—January 15—a federal holiday. The nation celebrates the life of Martin Luther King, Jr., because he helped his country to live up to its dream of equality for all.

Timetable of Events in the Life of Martin Luther King, Jr.

Jan 15, 1929	Born in Atlanta, Georgia
1947	Ordained Baptist minister
1948	Graduates from Morehouse College
1953	Marries Coretta Scott
1954	Becomes pastor of Dexter Avenue Baptist Church in Montgomery, Alabama
1955	Awarded Ph.D. in theology from Boston University
	Elected president of Montgomery Improvement Association to lead bus boycott
1957	Elected president of Southern Christian Leadership Conference (SCLC)
1963	Heads Birmingham, Alabama, demonstrations
	Writes "Letter from a Birmingham Jail"
	Delivers "I Have a Dream" speech at March on Washington
1964	Awarded Nobel Peace Prize
1965	Heads Selma, Alabama, demonstrations and march to Montgomery
1966	Moves family to ghetto in Chicago, Illinois; leads demonstrations there
1967	Announces Poor People's Campaign
1968	Leads demonstration in Memphis, Tennessee
	Delivers "I've Been to the Mountaintop" speech
April 4, 1968	Assassinated in Memphis, Tennessee

SUGGESTED READING

*Clayton, Ed. *Martin Luther King: The Peaceful Warrior*. New York: Pocket Books, 1969.

*Davidson, Margaret. *I Have a Dream: The Story of Martin Luther King, Jr.* New York: Scholastic Inc., 1986.

Faber, Doris and Harold Faber. *Martin Luther King, Jr.* New York: Messner, 1986.

*Haskins, James. *The Life & Death of Martin Luther King, Jr.* New York: Lothrop, 1977.

Jakoubek, Robert. *Martin Luther King, Jr.* New York: Chelsea House, 1989.

King, Coretta Scott. *My Life with Martin Luther King, Jr.* New York: Holt, Rinehart & Winston, 1969.

King, Martin Luther, Jr. *Stride Toward Freedom*. New York: Ballantine Books, 1961.

King, Martin Luther, Jr. *Why We Can't Wait*. New York: New American Library, 1963.

McKissack, Patricia and Frederick McKissack. *The Civil Rights Movement in America from 1865 to the Present.* Chicago: Childrens Press, 1987.

*Milton, Joyce. *Marching to Freedom: The Story of Martin Luther King, Jr.* New York: Dell Publishing, 1987.

*Patterson, Lillie. *Coretta Scott King*. Champaign, Ill.: Garrard Publishing Company, 1977.

Patterson, Lillie. *Martin Luther King, Jr. & the Montgomery Bus Boycott.* New York, Facts on File, 1989.

*Peck, Ira. *The Life and Words of Martin Luther King, Jr.* New York: Scholastic Inc., 1968.

*Quayle, Louise. *Martin Luther King, Jr.: Dreams for a Nation*. New York: Fawcett Columbine, 1989.

Schulke, Flip. *Martin Luther King, Jr.: A Documentary ... Montgomery to Memphis.* New York: W. W. Norton, 1976.

*Readers of *Martin Luther King, Jr.: The Dream of Peaceful Revolution* will find these books particularly readable.

SOURCES

BOOKS

Abernathy, Ralph D. *And the Walls Came Tumbling Down*. New York: Harper & Row, 1989.

Branch, Taylor. *Parting the Waters: America in the King Years, 1954–63*. New York: Simon and Schuster, 1988.

Fairclough, Adam. *To Redeem the Soul of America: The Southern Christian Leadership Conference and Martin Luther King, Jr.* Athens, Georgia: University of Georgia Press, 1987.

Farmer, James. *Lay Bare the Heart: An Autobiography of the Civil Rights Movement.* New York: New American Library, 1985.

Garrow, David J. *Bearing the Cross: Martin Luther King, Jr., and the Southern Christian Leadership Conference*. New York: Vintage Books, 1988.

King, Martin Luther, Jr. *The Strength to Love*. New York: Harper & Row, 1963.

King, Martin Luther, Jr. *Stride Toward Freedom*. New York: Ballantine Books, 1961.

King, Martin Luther, Jr. *The Trumpet of Conscience*. New York: Harper & Row, 1967.

King, Martin Luther, Jr., *Where Do We Go From Here: Chaos or Community?* New York: Harper & Row, 1967.

King, Martin Luther, Jr. *Why We Can't Wait*. New York: New American Library, 1963.

Morris, Aldon D. *The Origins of the Civil Rights Movement: Black Communities Organizing for Change*. New York: The Free Press, 1984.

Oates, Stephen B. *Let the Trumpet Sound: The Life of Martin Luther King, Jr.* New York: New American Library, 1982.

Raines, Howell. *My Soul Is Rested: The Story of the Civil Rights Movement in the Deep South*. New York: Penguin Books, 1977.

Schulke, Flip, and Penelope McPhee. *King Remembered*. New York: Pocket Books, 1986.

Washington, James Melvin, ed. *A Testament of Hope: The Essential Writings of Martin Luther King, Jr.* New York: Harper & Row, 1986.

Williams, Juan. *Eyes on the Prize*. New York: Viking, 1987.

INDEX

About the Author

Della Rowland was born in Evansville, Indiana. After moving to New York City, she worked at *Ms.* magazine and was an editor for primary grades at Scholastic, Inc. She has written a dozen children's books, including a series on animals for early readers, a retelling of "Beauty and the Beast," and biographies of Sacajawea, a Shoshoni Indian woman, and Martin Luther King, Jr. She is a member of the Authors Guild.

Picture Credits: A. Philip Randolph Institute: 29; AP/Wide World Photos: 16, 38, 49, 53, 90, 91, 99, 106; Bert Miles: cover background; Black Star: cover portrait; Sam Falk/NYT Pictures: 116; Schomburg Center for Research in Black Culture, N.Y. Public Library, Astor, Lenox and Tilden Foundations: 6, 28, 67, 88, 98, 121, 125, 127; Flip Schulke: 78.